START
FOR
SUCCESS

JAN
CAVELLE

Start For Success by Jan Cavelle

First published by Glennon-Anderson Publishing, 2022

Copyright © 2022 by Jan Cavelle.

ISBN: 978-1-7391910-0-9

Cover design and interior design by Paul Palmer-Edwards

Start for Success is dedicated to my son, Jack, who coached me through the brick-wall moment, when I completely doubted my ability to go ahead. He grows as a person year in year out and I could not be more proud of him.

What readers have said about *Start For Success*

"Where was this book when I needed it?! When I started my first company this book would have been invaluable. It is packed with practical advice that I had to learn through trial and error. A lot of time wasted. I am going to bulk buy and hand out to any new entrepreneurs on my mentorship program."
Rachel Watkyn. Founder, Tiny Box Company

"This book reveals what it is really like — and what it really takes — to create and grow a successful start-up. Practical, jargon-free and easy to digest. It's a fascinating read with actionable tips you can use on your business. I wish I had this book when I started out on my entrepreneurial journey 25 years ago!"
Steve Bolton. Founder & Group CEO , Bolt Partners

"There are many books written about starting and growing a business, so what makes this one different?
   Here, Jan has really broken the wider subject down into focussed areas on specific topics in a way that is very readable. So, whether you read it cover-to-cover or dip in when you need some direction, you'll find good advice illustrated with real-life, relatable stories. This book sweeps away the mystery and enigma surrounding entrepreneurship and replaces it with practical guidance and insights."
Duane Jackson. Serial entrepreneur

"Jan Cavelle has pulled together the most comprehensive, practical 'how to' guide for founders... Every founder will find something useful in it."
Ben Legg. Co-founder, Portfolio Collective

"These pages remind us that start-up success doesn't happen overnight. Cavelle's collection of founder-stories from all over the world live-out the strikingly relatable challenges and joys of starting a business. An inspiring and comforting reminder that 'big things' come in time and sometimes to start, it's all about finding a way to keep the lights on and make enough room for the next step."
Nicholas Schooling. Co-Founder, Local Knowledge Travel

"Compelling stories and practical lesson make Start for Success a great read for entrepreneurs at any stage. The key business knowledge combined with people's real stories makes it easy to understand and later apply the concepts. A must have book for anyone thinking of starting a business or who's already started."
Karla Garza. Director, Key Coworking

"This book reminds us, story-by-story, that we are all entrepreneurs. Many times, our passion to create remains locked in dreams as opposed to reality and this thoughtfully curated compilation of real-life experiences by Cavelle facilitates a deep understanding of the shared challenges and fear that exist for founders everywhere. A must-read for any entrepreneur; "Start for Success" lights the spark of confidence needed to cross the line of fear, and step into an adventurous world of business possibilities that could benefit generations of the future.

By demonstrating the grit, determination, focus and hard work it has taken successful founders to get to get to where they want to be, "Start for Success" touches on a multitude of useful everyday tools to help new founders get ideas off the ground, and guide established business owners in building on success."
Philip Dumont de Chassart. CEO, Balu Pecan & Chairman, Surrey Group

"I would recommend that if you're thinking of starting a business the first step you need to take would be to read this book... A great read on the struggles and achievement that every business has from day to day."
Niall Greenan. Founder, Greenan Products: The Smart Bunker

"The book reminded me of my days as a SaaS founder and now as a start-up mentor. It's a comprehensive presentation by Jan Cavelle, covering every aspect of the business, and what can be expected. With every page turn, I felt like my experience had been succinctly documented to be shared with the world - which shows that despite our belief that our situations are unique, they are not dissimilar.

In addition to sparking a few new ideas, the stories I read from fellow founders made me rethink the way I approach mentorship and building my own business. From conception to initial public offering, this book provides a bird's eye view of what Founders can expect at every stage, and a few antidotes for good measure."
Keshni Morar. Serial entrepreneur/mentor/investor, Investable Business

"Start for Success is the book I wish I had when I was starting out on my journey. It would have saved me so much time, money, and energy with its wisdom."

There are so many great takeaways from this book that even a few years into my journey have helped me pivot my thinking into more successful ways of doing!!"
Kylee Leota. Director & Chief Vision Officer, Elements 4 Success

"Jan has a phenomenal grasp of the practical side of running and building a business. This book inspires and motivates while also hitting the rare practical advice that is easy to grasp and follow. I'm impressed."
Stephanie Scheller. Founder, Grow Disrupt

"The depth and breadth of knowledge represented in this book is surprisingly substantial. Extremely well researched, but reads lightly and quickly, as any essential book about business should. A must read for entrepreneurs that they'll actually be able to get through, with stories they'll instantly recognize and identify with."
Hiram Skaggs. VP, FunAndMoving.com

This book includes stories from the following entrepreneurs

USA
Abe Matamoros, EllieGrid
Chad Wasilenkoff, Helicoid
   Industries
Daniel Koffler, New Frontiers
Dr Jeff Chen, Radicle Science
Dr Wei-Shin Lai, AccousticSheep
Elnaz Sarraf, ROYBI Robot
Glen Bhimani, BPS Security
Jarie Bolander,
   The Entrepeneur Ethos
Kalyan Gautham, WATT
Richard Boyd, Tanjo.AI
Stephen Halasnik, Financing
   Solutions

Australia
Andrew Barnes, Go1
Craig Dempsey, BLH
Daniel Flynn, Thankyou
David Jenyns, Systemology
Jake Munday, Custom Neon
Jeremy Fleming, Stagekings
Mark Allen, Patch
Matt Bullock, Spinify
Michael Holmstrom, STEM Punks
Sharon Melamed, Matchboard
Shem Richards, Goldilocks Suit
Tony Nicholls, Good Talent Media

Canada
Harold Punnet, NervGen

France
Nicolas Naigeon, AVEiNE
Roger Jackson, Shopper Intelligence

Switzerland
Ben Talin, 361consult

United Kingdom
Andrey Yashunsky, Prytek
Asim Amin, Plumm
Bhairav Patel, Atom Ventures
Calypso Rose, Indytute
Charlie Cook, Rightcharge
Charlotte Pearce, Inkpact
Craig Bunting, BEAR
Craig Knight, Identity Realization
Damian Connolly, Sakura Business
   Solutions
Danny Matthews, Brand specialist
Deepak Shukla, Pearl Lemon Group
Emma Parkinson, International
   Energy Products
George Rawlings, Thursday
Georgia Metcalfe, French Bedroom
   Company
Gordon Midwood, Anything World

Ian Finch, Click Europe
Jade Francine, WeMaintain
Jamie Irwin, Straight Up Search
Jazz Gill, SPARBAR
Jenni Field, Redefining
  Communications
Jeremie Warner, Power a Life
Jessica Flinn, Jessica Flinn Design
Joe Seddon, Zero Gravity
Julie Bishop, IT Naturally
Laura Harnett, The Seep Company
Lina Barker, Aaron Wallace
Lucy Gordon, From Our Cellar
Mark Hayward, Sway PR
Matt Leach, Geotekk
Olly Richards, StoryLearning
Olivia James, The Harley Street
  Coach
Paris Michailidis, My Little Panda
Paul Brown, BOL
Rich Wilson, Gigged.AI
Richard Mabey, Juro Online
Richard Osborne, UK Business
  Forums
Roger Jackson, Shopper Intelligence
Roman Grigoriev, Boomf & Splento
Rune Sovndahl, Fantastic Services
Sanjay and Shashi Aggarwhal,
  The Spice Kitchen

Tim Mercer, Vapour
Tom Mills, Two Oceans Strategy
Vicky Whiter, Peters' Cleaners
Wilfred Emmanuel Jones, The Black
  Farmer

Contents

Introduction

If you have picked up this book, you are probably either thinking about or already starting a business. And you want it to grow, fast.

Starting a business is one of the most exciting things you can do. But you may be unsure of a few things, a bit frightened even – that is where I come in. I am a colossal champion of entrepreneurs. I genuinely think you are all amazing, and with nearly four decades under my belt of founding and running small businesses, I understand a bit about what works and what doesn't too.

Entrepreneurship in the Pandemic

Along with most people, in the spring of 2019, I felt like the proverbial Alice. As a writer, an entrepreneur, and an individual, it was akin to falling down the rabbit hole – and emerging in some dystopian land where nothing was the same.

What gradually re-installed some optimism came from the entrepreneurs I spoke to. As always, extraordinary, innovative, adaptable, courageous... the majority were meeting the new challenges head on, and were determined to adapt and survive against new odds.

Over the course of several decades, I have been involved in campaigns to support entrepreneurs. I have always believed that if I can pass on a piece of knowledge, make a difference to one of you entrepreneurs out there, contribute a bit of wisdom to help you on your journey and some inspiration to help you keep trying... then that is indeed worthwhile.

Changes in the entrepreneurial world

Scale for Success, my first book, was going through its final edits as the pandemic hit. The contributing entrepreneurs shared invaluable wisdom, much of which is still relevant after the pandemic. But I was soon aware that a positive volcano of new trends was erupting. Tech is estimated to have advanced forty years within the first two years of the pandemic alone. While that leaves some entrepreneurs effervescent about the opportunities, others are floundering and out of their depth. Before the pandemic, only a few people had heard of the metaverse, NFTs or blockchain. For the non-techie entrepreneurs among you, that can be scary.

There is the great resignation, with more of you wanting to take control and start businesses, and the introduction of home working and hybrid working – which may or may not suit you. On top of that, there's uncertainty by the bucket load, supply-chain challenges abound, inflation is rocketing, and that is to say nothing of the impact on mental health! We are going to help with all of these.

Opportunities abound:

The situation is far from being all doom and gloom. Amongst the disruption, opportunity is there for your taking. We have learned to innovate on an unprecedented scale, and the world of entre-preneurship generally is booming, sometimes in areas we could not have predicted a few years ago.

Industries associated with hospitality, for example, were decimated during the first lockdowns. As a result, companies commonly lost between 70-100% of their business overnight. There must have been moments of panic, yet incredibly resourceful entrepreneurs regrouped and looked for new avenues and opportunities.

Many of them did even better than before. Some pivoted from B2B to direct to customer or set up home-delivery services. Others varied what they did. For example, I have talked to the ever-growing groups of non-alcohol drinks companies which, as a result of the escalation in focus on wellness, have hit a seam of unprecedented growth. I spoke to an events company who pivoted over a single weekend to become a successful furniture manufacturer, keeping their staff's skill sets in use (read how they did it later). How inspirational is that?

As burnout and stress have understandably rocketed, so have companies offering help in this space, from online workshops and counsellors to self-help apps. With medical services harder to access, new telemedical services have mushroomed. Teachers, tutors, and specialists met the demands of parents, individuals and companies by going online instead. Cleaning companies have increased their skill set to offer deep cleaning.

When the world shut down, we saw animals thrive, from Pumas in South America, wild boar in Barcelona and goats on the high streets of North Wales. Within a few weeks of lockdown, The Ganges, one of the world's most polluted rivers started to clear, and even become drinkable for the first time in two decades. While there might be some animals we don't want to meet when picking up a loaf of bread, more and more people are becoming aware of the damage we have done to the planet and want to change things for the better. Entrepreneurs are leaders in this, adapting and embracing it. More and more businesses are committed to making the world a better place. Increasing numbers believe that the future holds fundamental economic changes, that growth is unsustainable for its own sake as the planet will simply run out of resources. They believe that businesses of the future will focus less on financial return and more on impact and its impact on the quality of our lives.

At long last, sustainability is at the front of the agenda.

Be a part of the entrepreneur tribe!

The lovely, positive feedback I got from my first book, Scale for Success, noted that it was a different type of business book. The stories, messages and points of learning came from real entrepreneurs who know from personal experiences all the struggles you are going through. I was over the moon to find it so well received.

I have always been a massive fan of peer learning, and that is what I aim to recreate when I write. For example, someone described reading the book as spending an "exceptionally good evening brainstorming with other entrepreneurs a bit further on the journey than I am." If you would find that of benefit, read on.

We will journey through most of the many aspects needed for early start-up for growth together, with stories from many brilliant and experienced global entrepreneurs. I hope you will feel immediately at home in this tribe, recognize the struggles and experiences that they share in their anecdotes, and know that you share a journey and belong.

It is a tough, challenging, nail-biting roller-coaster of a ride with too high a proportion of people falling off. I don't want you to be the one of those people that procrastinates or stumbles! I want you to start with impact, developing your life, your customers, perhaps the planet, whatever does it for you. I want you to succeed in launching and growing.

I want to flag up possible dangers, inspire you with stories, and take you on a journey through the new world of entrepreneurship. We will look at the reasons to do it, creating value, building a team, building a sustainable business - a massive range of things that will leave you a little bit wiser at the end, and with a better chance of succeeding.

And as a bonus, I hope to entertain you along the way, as some of the awesome entrepreneurs that appear in the book have certainly entertained and inspired me. You will learn how Bear Grylls helped one entrepreneur close down businesses that weren't working or how another had their business brainwave whilst struggling for breath at the top of a mountain. Listen to another pitching in a deckchair on the pavement outside his house; find out how buzz marketing and homemade sandwich boards can bring thousands of downloads, how to pivot your business in a weekend, raise investment by asking people to drop their trousers or protect your team when a customer threatens to "Uzi them"!

These are true entrepreneurs' stories, in every shape and size, from garage start-ups that have gone global, to some that are a little earlier on their journey. All are wonderfully honest about the experiences they went through and the mistakes they made.

The Future

The entrepreneurs in the book will bring the journey alive for you and share many ideas to inspire you to find new solutions as you move forward into your new and incredibly exciting future.

Some chapters will inspire you; others will deliver a barrage of actionable tips that you can apply right now.

I genuinely believe entrepreneurs will lead the way forward, creating new jobs and a better future. If you are only just starting your high-growth journey or already a little way in, I applaud you. You are amazing.

SECTION ONE

Why Do It?

Running your own business is a challenging thing to do. There is a heap of pros but they are not always what people expect. The freedom people seek does usually appear at least to some extent - until you start to employ people. Hard work there will still be. The dreams of riches come true less often and definitely not in the early stages. Other rewards may or may not come further down the road.

Yet the majority of founders are addicted to their businesses, despite the challenges. The reason for that nearly always lies in the "why" behind their choice to do it. That "why" is what will inspire you, keep you going when things get rough, and get you leaping out from under the duvet, however miserable the day.

In this section, we look at different "whys". For some people, these are altruistic, for others practical and sometimes a way to live life on your terms and by your values. We will also look at sustainability, something high on many of our minds now.

Whatever your reasons, you need something to aim for and a method of getting there, so we also look at missions, visions, goals and business planning.

CHAPTER ONE

Burning Whys

The last decade or so has seen a massive growth of the burning "why" entrepreneurs. These are people on a mission to improve the planet or the lives of those who live on it. These people become so passionate about what they want to change, that their only option is to start a business.

You cannot invent or adopt these sorts of "whys". They have to come from deep within you, and powered by a force and a determination that is unarguable. Not all of us has a why like this, and there are many other good reasons to start and grow a business, but the burning wouldn't-be-doing-it-otherwise sort of whys are unique.

Sometimes, these entrepreneurs create businesses to solve a problem directly, creating companies that work on changing the problem itself. Others create a different business but through the way it is run, make changes to lives and the planet. We see more and more people dedicating themselves to make the world a better place.

These burning whys can move mountains and I am sharing a couple of stories here to show you what is possible.

Two Daft Laddies

By his own description, Jeremie Warner and his original co-founder were just, "a couple of daft laddies from Glasgow". As part of his training to be an architect, Jeremie worked on a building job in Singapore. They were creating houses for multi-millionaires, yet Jeremie could see that the people working on the site had no shoes. The contrast sickened him.

Jeremie returned to Glasgow and changed the Master's he was studying to a social one, choosing to do a dissertation in Senegal. Jeremie spent some time there, studying what impacted people's lives the most. He found out for himself how hard life was in Senegal, following a tribal dinner and some dubious tripe that led to him being taken to the health centre on a drip, on the back of a donkey cart.

The villages had no electricity. It was a 40 km round trip to power up Jeremie's laptop and the lack of electricity had a more significant impact: there was no light once the sun had gone down. Jeremie realized that when his child cried at night in Glasgow, he could put on a light, yet this was a luxury none of these parents had. Schooling and homework were restricted, impacting long-term education and having knock-on effects that lasted for the rest of their lives.

Jeremie's solution was to start a mobile phone accessories company called Power a Life. With every product they sell, they give a free solar light to a child in a developing country. For every child they empower, family members also benefit from solar lighting. While they had to reduce their targets during the pandemic, they still aim to have empowered 10,000 children by 2022.

It is still a phenomenal impact from one single entrepreneur. Yet Jeremie was not qualified in business, and his journey has been fraught with problems. At the start, their first investment deal collapsed, and they had to close the company. His original co-founder dropped out, but Jeremie kept going solo, maintaining an income by driving a pizza van till he could revive his dream. There are easier ways to make money, but it was never about that. His burning "why" kept him going.

A story of tragedy, hope, and a dream

Canadian entrepreneur Harold Punnett DMD describes the origins of his business as "a story of tragedy, a hope, and a dream, and one for which the end is yet to be written."

In March 2016, his daughter-in-law, Codi, suffered a tragic fall and became a complete T-11 paraplegic. At only 29 years old, she had lost all movement and sensation below her belly button. It was a devastating time for her and her husband, Ian, and their three young children. They were all in a state of shock, and Harold says that he would find himself wandering the house at 3 a.m.

In a moment of clarity, he spoke what he was thinking aloud, "I have to fix this, I have to help Codi." He knew it was crazy, but he felt compelled to try.

Despite the hour of the night, he went to his computer and typed "spinal cord injury" into the search engine. Harold has a medical background that made accessing the science easier and he deep-dived, contacting scientists all over the world. He knew that potential investors would not be interested in anything without a short-term return. Harold had, therefore, set criteria to find revolutionary solutions that were only years, not decades away. Results were profoundly discouraging.

After extensive searching, Harold found the technology in the research of Dr. Jerry Silver of Case Western Reserve University. He had discovered what they now know to be the prime inhibitor of nerve repair after injury and how to turn that inhibitor off. Harold quickly realized this discovery's potential to help with neurodegenerative diseases and injuries such as SCI, MS, strokes, traumatic brain injury and peripheral nerve injury, Alzheimer's, and more.

Within four years, Harold founded a start-up, NervGen Pharma, raised the investment, and NervGen's lead product soon went into clinical trials. Harold says that during the last five years, he has learned that the impossible is not in fact impossible and dreams can become reality. He has discovered that it is possible to inspire others to see your vision, and together, perhaps change the future of millions of people.

Whys that make the Impossible Possible

These are two very different people and two very different stories. Jeremie created a product from which he could fund solutions to the problem. Harold set out to tackle his problem directly. Both leapt into fields they knew little or nothing about, but neither of them stopped – not even for an instant. Their determination to change lives was so strong that they set out to achieve the impossible without a second thought. They were not deterred when setbacks hit; their goals were so important that they did not waiver.

Even if you are an entrepreneur with a mission that is that important to you, obstacles are not necessarily easy to overcome – but your perseverance and determination to succeed are what gives you the strength to do just that. They give you that belief.

While every little bit helps, the more you succeed with your business, the more positive impact you will have on others and the planet, and the greater good you can achieve.

CHAPTER TWO

Other Whys

Most entrepreneurs do not have a burning "why." But there are many other very good reasons to start a business.

The old definition of an entrepreneur as someone who starts a business and takes on financial risk in the hope of profit falls short. The opportunity has to be worth the risk, but even more importantly, so do your reasons, altruistic or otherwise. And these have to be grounded in your personal truth.

A word of warning though – do not start a business just to get rich. It is easy to get blinded by money and believe it will bring happiness, especially when you are broke and unhappy. But of course, this is a misconception. Real wealth comes from a life that is in balance, a life of family, friends and things that bring you joy. To achieve that, we only need to take acute money worries off the table. The reason for founding a business has to be more profound than just money. Money alone will not get you out of bed, or keep you going when things get tough.

Necessity is a Great Motivator

Sometimes, the reasons we start businesses are simple. We do it for our families. When I first became a single mum, I decided to work at home so that I could look after the children at the same time. It was not just about putting food on the table, though that was crucial. It was also about creating a lifestyle that enabled me to be around to look after them, rather than leaving them with a childminder while I went out to work every day. Later on, when I got the business off the ground, I realized I might be able to give the children opportunities they wouldn't otherwise have had. However, the "what" I was doing, the type of business, was immaterial, providing I could achieve that.

Single parents everywhere are driven by the need to provide for their children. With a combination of the great resignation and innumerable redundancies happening worldwide, many new entrepreneurs will be forming businesses out of the need to feed their families. They might be side hustles or full-time hustles. Either way, necessity is indeed a great big mother of invention.

What I quickly found out is that the people you work with also give you a secondary drive. We initially created a great atmosphere, a fun place where we worked hard but enjoyed being there, and creating a special place to work was great motivation in itself. Finding a tribe or community is something that we are intrinsically geared for and something else that can give you a strong why, be it with the people you work with or the places you create.

Another reason is to provide something missing in your life – be it a problem you couldn't find the solution for, or a community you want to be a part of.

Business Communities

Richard Osborne had a troubled childhood, got into drugs, and had anger-management issues, smashing up the family home when he was 16. Someone found him a place on a training scheme. At first, Richard says he was still getting high every lunchtime, but slowly he started to realize the work and effort that the owner of the business was putting in, in order to give them all jobs. As Richard's work improved, he earned a pay rise and a promotion, and started to work his way out of trouble.

Then things went wrong: the family home was repossessed. Richard lived briefly on his aunt's floor before moving in with his girlfriend's family, and this experience of a happy family environment brought back Richard's anger. But this time, he worked things through, until he and his girlfriend had a home of their own.

That family community had stabilized Richard, and when he later started a business of his own, he felt the isolation keenly. He missed office camaraderie, peers to run ideas past, and people to brainstorm and share experiences with. Convinced that other founders must have the same issues, and passionately believing that success and happiness is found within communities, Richard co-founded UK Business Forums, which was an online networking group that would become the UK's most active online community for small- and micro-business owners. Going from a simple "why" of helping himself and others, Richard has expanded the community and represents small businesses in Whitehall and beyond.

Local Communities

Craig Bunting, founder of the multi-site coffee brand, BEAR, had spent time in Australia and sorely missed the socializing style of their cafés and bars, which are the hub of local communities. In the UK, the concept of a casual, all day dining café or bar as a local meeting place simply didn't exist outside of London. He and his business partner, Michael Thorley, saw a gap in the market and decided to open a café where they, friends, and like-minded people could hang out as a community. BEAR works on the principle that sharing life is always better and good things happen over a cup of coffee. It worked so well that they now have many hugely popular sites across the Midlands and Cheshire, alongside a successful online store selling coffee and sustainable lifestyle products.

These are very different stories, but what unites them is the desire of the entrepreneurs that made them happen: the desire to build the sort of life they wanted to lead, with the sort of community they wanted to be a part of.

The Desire to Create

Another commonality with entrepreneurs is a love of bringing things to life. This includes both their businesses and what they offer. As it was with me, what you are breathing life into may not be as important as that act of creation.

Founders are quickly caught up in the need to build, and I believe that need is one of the secret sauces that keeps us entrepreneurs going. We have ideas, see opportunities, and want to make them fly. You may have that niggling feeling now, that need to build.

Founders are quickly caught up in the need to build, and I believe that need is one of the secret sauces that keeps us entrepreneurs going. We have ideas, see opportunities, and want to make them fly. You may have that niggling feeling now, that need to build.

When I interviewed the hugely successful American entrepreneur Alyson Watson for my website's entrepreneur interview series, she told me her story. She had always dreamed of starting her own business. Everyone had told her that she would need to be in Silicon Valley if she wanted to do it. Eventually, the desire to create became so great that she bought a one-way ticket to San Francisco.

Rob Hamilton, one of the entrepreneurs in Scale for Success, carried a notebook around with him for a few years, noting ideas down so that he could assess them and see if they would fly.

For some, it is the passion to create a business that is the personal truth behind starting up. The passion for what you do and why you do it have to come from you, the founder, – and to be successful, that passion has to be both completely authentic and deeply personal.

CHAPTER THREE

Breathing Life into your Brand

You may know why you are doing what you do – but to really bring it to life, you have to set out where you are going and why. Communicating to the people who work for you, the people who invest in you, your customers and other stakeholders exactly what you are all about is a crucial part of what you do as a leader and entrepreneur. Expressing it can start with something as simple your business name.

This is how Australian social enterprise Thankyou breathed life into their brand and how they put their impact at the heart of their vision.

Thankyou

Thankyou was founded by the then 19-year-old Daniel Flynn, his now-wife, Justine Flynn, and their best friend, Jarryd Burns. The founders wanted to launch a business that would benefit people on a lasting basis rather than start a company with a goodwill extra or a marketing strategy that would include some give-back. They wanted impact to be the entire purpose of their business.

They launched in 2008 with an initial product of bottled water.

An early challenge was to settle on a brand name with the power to match the impact they were aiming for. Daniel had a clear image in his head of a boy drinking water from a bottle and could see the words "thankyou" written across the image. Having found a similar image online, he then placed "thankyou", written as one word, across it.

For a moment, they wondered if they could call a product "thankyou," but they did, and their conviction paid off.

A vision from there

There are approximately 736 million people in extreme poverty. By 2030, the funding gap to end extreme poverty is estimated to be 2.5 trillion US dollars a year. Meanwhile, consumer spending totals around 63 trillion US dollars a year. The contrast is appalling, and it was this disparity that the Thankyou founders wanted to change.

Their vision, how they want things to be as a result of their social enterprise, was "To see a world where no-one person lives in extreme poverty."

Visions are your baselines

Visions are different from missions and goals are different from missions. Goals are something you achieve, before moving on to the next one. You don't aim to end world poverty, do so and then say, "great, done that, now I am going to do something else and not care if everyone starves". A vision describes the state you want to get to and then maintain. As entrepreneurs, we all sometimes feel out of control, but your vision will keep you grounded.

Your vision ripples through your entire business. It impacts your values and team choices, and it defines your culture. A purely self-serving one won't work. Imagine the headline "I will be a billionaire and have seven houses". Will it inspire customers to buy or people to work alongside you to achieve such a vision? Of course not.

But when you have a vision supported by values that other people identify with, then you have the start of your tribe. A group of people with the same values and vision creates the momentum to move towards success.

Visions and Missions

Having defined a mission as Thankyou did, the question you should be asking yourself is how you are going to achieve it. For example, for Thank you, their mission is "Amplifying impactful change-makers to better serve people living in extreme poverty by redistributing wealth from consumer spending." That started with offering consumer products that people love to use and encouraging people everywhere to choose Thankyou, which has now grown to be one of Australia's most prominent social enterprises.

If visions are the big picture outcomes you are striving towards, your mission is the "how" you are getting there. Visions, the ways we want the world to look as a result, tend to remain unchanged. However, if you want to "see a world where no one lives in poverty", ways of working towards that goal might, over the years, change.

Just as the vision has to get people excited, so does the mission. The link to how it will move you forward towards the vision, the shift the mission will make, has to be absolutely clear to people so they can be inspired.

For example, suppose your vision is to create "a sustainable world". In that case, you might have a mission of "making EVs affordable for everyone", but equally, you might be on a mission to "revolutionize salt-water farming".

Visions, and indeed missions, are easily aspirational if they improve the lives of others, particularly if they are based around issues that many people are extremely passionate about, such as sustainability.

But what do you do if you have a more prosaic product with a less immediately inspirational goal? You can still aim to change people's lives, make them happier, solve their problems, and give them something they love. Remember Craig Bunting in Chapter Two, transforming coffee shops into hubs for communities to meet up, spend time together, and drink exceptional coffee. Still changing lives for the better.

Business Planning

Your vision is your dream and will almost certainly take years or even decades to bring to life. Your mission is how you are going there at the moment, and that may well get updated every so often. Business plans are something else altogether.

Luckily, when it comes to business plans, the colossal monsters that the banks used to demand have become extinct. There are two excellent reasons for that: one is that while the bank insisted on these plans, once done, they would fester in a bottom drawer because they were too cumbersome to use. Secondly, business has become faster and faster evolving. This means that plans have to be agile, brief, easy to use, and easy to update.

Of course, you need a good strategy to achieve a trajectory that will lead to fast growth. The easiest way to do that is to look at the end point of your mission: what are the resources that your mission demands, and what income would that generate (and is that a healthy enough outcome – check!) Then work backwards from there.

- What would that look like halfway, or a quarter of the way there?
- How much would that cost at those points?
- What other resources would the business need?

Look at those costs, add in a cash-flow runway and extra money for the unexpected, and you can start to put together a forecast of what you will need to raise at various stages. It is that simple, and it should be easy enough for you to understand and achieve. You can always get a financial whizz to lay it out in a way that impresses investors, but it is you as a founder that has to use it, control it and understand it.

Assuming you then have your cash-flow plan and financing worked out (lots of help with that later), then it is always the next quarter that requires detailed planning. Look at your overall summary to see what those key deliverables are in terms of sales and costs, and working with teams in each area, set goals for how you will all achieve them. Continually evaluate how you are doing: adjust and achieve. These are your goals, and each area of the business should have its own goals that help it to measure its contribution to the quarterly goals of the business as a whole. Keep it simple. If everyone understands where they are going and why, they can get on board with it.

The better your systems for monitoring, the easier it will be. If you find something goes wildly wrong you can quickly leap on it, re-evaluate, and change things to make it work. A plan like this is an invaluable tool, but don't let it dominate your life and be ready to throw it out of the window if things change. It's crucial to flex when you need to.

The Secret

The secret to success doesn't lie in enormously complex plans, but it is still often missed. The secret lies in the timing. If, for example, when you look at your situation at the next halfway point to your overall mission and see that you will need x financing and y people, the idea is not to end up organizing things with a week to go.

Successful entrepreneurs have those things in place ready so that growth is never held up by a lack of resources. How simple (or complex) those resources are to get hold of influences when you will need to start organizing them. A senior member of staff takes considerable time to find and embed, and financing takes time – different amounts of time, depending on the type. Your job is to ensure it is all there ready.

B Plans

Something else I found essential is a B Plan. This B plan isn't about the predictable risks, which we will discuss later. This B Plan s because you may want out of that business sooner than expected.

There can be many reasons for this, such as illness, burnout or a change in personal circumstances. For many years, I would sit in my office and hold forth about how I would be in my last business till I dropped because I loved it so much. But for whatever reason, as I found out, there can come a day when you don't love it, or that you do but accept it is time to move on. Life is full of the unexpected.

Plan Bs have two vital parts. The first premise is never to invest every penny into that business but instead draw reasonable amounts of money out, and invest it for your future so that you are never left penniless at the end of years of hard graft. Do not tell yourself that you are building your future by giving the business your financial support: that is to risk everything on one horse.

The second is to ensure that your business is sellable at all times. Firstly, this means learning how to sell a company, something that is neither hard nor expensive, yet many entrepreneurs are scared of it, and instead pay experts, and get fleeced. The second part means good housekeeping, in the form of excellent paperwork and sound systems. It means being solvent with a solid client base so someone else would benefit from having the business. It means moving to a stage where the company is not reliant on you. Until then, it will be of little or no value to anyone else.

CHAPTER FOUR

Values are a way of life

Values are what you stand for. They are your brand's personality, the way you live life and a great asset in deciding everything you do. They give you purpose, guide what you do, and bind you to partners, suppliers, and your team.

Let's look at how values work best and their impact.

Creating a personality

The stronger and more individual your branding is, the more you will stand out. The character needs to zing and be recognizable instantly. But more than that, everything has to be underpinned by the strong values behind your company.

Imagine you are bringing a character in a book you are writing alive. You would want the reader to know what the character looks like, what they think, what they feel, but also why they think and feel that way. That is what makes one person different from another. Half-hearted values are unmemorable; for example:

- We aim to be good
- We try and do right
- We do our best for customers
- We want to make people happy.

They tell us nothing at all about that brand's personality and wouldn't get anyone excited. Completely grey and washed out. Replace those with:

- Aim to be best
- Put others first
- Make our customers smile
- Spread joy.

They aren't fully developed but you already start to get a sense of what matters to the people involved and why they do what they do.

Values may include how you view what you actually do, where you want the company to move towards, and what you want your social effect to be. Each area can be equally important. We will look at that more shortly. Just as a person can be innovative, ambitious and passionate about sustainability, they don't contradict but make up a whole picture.

It is easy to get tempted to write long, waffling sentences. If you are talking about a character, you could say, "they walked up a hill, down a hill, and then another 25 miles," or you could just say they completed a marathon. Which will people remember? And it is all about memorability. The shorter the value, the stronger, the easier to remember.

One to four words is plenty. If, for example, innovation is a crucial value, it will not be more effective if you water it down to "innovation with our products" or "innovation at work". A single word really is all that is needed.

Just as the wording of your values should be short, I have found that a small quantity works best too. The more there are, the harder for anyone to remember. They cannot ever be token words but have to be what really underlines how you run your company. They are the cornerstone of why you make your decisions, checking if they are in keeping with your values. They are what make you decide that one person will fit when someone else won't when recruiting one person, or what makes you choose one supplier to another of equal quality and price?

Your values should be the reason behind why you and everyone involved behaves the way they do and interacts the way they do with others, both within and outside the company.

When a company acts against its own values, it confuses and alienates. Most importantly, it destroys trust. One example is green-washing, of course, when a company puts sustainability at the top of its values. Then it is found to be doing something with a heinous effect on the environment. Instantly, all trust is obliterated.

If you are still unsure, try looking up some of your favourite brands' values. See if you think they express personality, if you would remember them, and if your dealings with that company have reflected those values.

Values influence how the company behaves much more than you can imagine. Years ago, a company I started had "fun" as one of its values. Later we changed it to something more serious. And everyone slowly stopped having fun.

Types of Value

Values fall into different categories. Firstly, there are personality values, human traits and behaviours of how people representing the business act. Examples might be excellence, humility, or patience. Then there are the ones surrounding how the business aims to perform, which might include growth and quality or doing the right thing.

You might choose values surrounding how you make customers feel, from delivering excellent service or simply making them happy. The next group is about how you interact with people; not just

customers. but everyone – team members, stakeholders and collab-
orators. Examples here might be respect, compassion, or loyalty.

Finally, there are values to do with your impact on your immediate
or broader community, and these include sustainability, being
environmentally-conscious, or giving back to the local community.

In whittling down the quantity, you can ensure you don't have
two that are similar.

There is also an argument for prioritizing values, asking your-
selves which ones really matter the most when it counts. What is
right for one company, might not be right for another. For example,
a construction company might choose this order:

1. Safety
2. Sustainability
3. Equality
4. Learning

Who should write them?

Some founders write their values, and then some take them to
the team for input. I would strongly suggest against giving the
whole decision over to your team, especially as the business grows.
That gut North Star link to what matters should always stay true.
No founder can put in the heart and soul that's needed to get a
business off the ground unless they identify 110% with the values
of that business.

Not everyone is as central in the decisions. If you already have
very senior management in place, then absolutely involve them.
In fact, that is important, as that original core team need to be
entirely committed to the values so that these values will be more
easily retained as you grow. For example, when used in recruitment,

you will naturally attract and select people who will fit and make decisions in keeping with the values, thus building a solid culture that everyone is aligned with and committed to. You can find an example of this in the chapter 'recruitment for growth', which shows how values underline the culture needed for success.

One problem is that many companies employ marketing, PR or even HR companies to write values that will make them look good and develop a particular brand image. These specialists may create what looks like an appealing brand from the outside, but they won't be authentically yours nor come from the guts or the heart. They will be meaningless to you and meaningless to your team – and because of that, they will never work.

There is no "ought to be" in values

Julie Bishop had a baptism of fire when she took up her role as CEO of IT Naturally. Julie had worked in aviation, holding high-ranking positions in major airlines running IT infrastructures. However, when Thomas Cook went into insolvency, she was offered the chance to take over a major German airline's IT support in an attempt to save the business. Overnight, after 30 years in the corporate world, never having dreamed of being an entrepreneur, she found herself with a 3 million pound contract and 28 employees.

Julie says that the first year was spent achieving the impossible for their new customer, and it took time to adjust to being a new CEO. She had become accustomed to having sizeable organizational support teams. Now, there was no one behind her and her husband and partner, who, Julie says, was walking past the kitchen table at the wrong moment and got pulled in to help.

Her corporate background brought strengths. She introduced internal processes and controls, which quickly won the company ISO ratings and an Investors in People accreditation. She loved the freedom to do things "her way" and treat people in the way she wanted. For example, a few months in, she sent all her team's children a personally signed letter saying, "Thank you for letting your Mummy/Daddy work for us".

Both Julie and her partner realized that their weakest areas were sales and marketing so they sought out a specialist business coach. Julie recalls that the first few sessions were horrendous, as they started to see the gap between what they wanted to say about the company and the message that their website and marketing was communicating. Julie says that being from an IT background, she is very fact-driven, and their communications were missing any emotional connection in the company's personality.

They had chosen values for the company, which Julie describes as precisely what they thought the values "ought" to be. These values resonated with no one, and they quickly learned these needed to be as honest and individual as the letters they had written to their team's children.

IT Naturally's values have changed to:

- Humancentric
- Dedicated
- Playful

Playful is the one that takes people by surprise. It is not what is expected from an IT company. Yet it feels entirely the right choice to Julie and her team, and her customers all say so as well. It is their natural language, not someone else's, and the values are authentic.

CHAPTER FIVE

Sustainability

I first heard about sustainability over two decades ago. I was still in manufacturing, and I quickly saw that the days of doing things with the processes we were using were numbered. The question was what to do about it. I started with our supply chain and was impressed to discover that our chemical suppliers were already all over it. Providing we invested in some expensive machinery, we could adapt the processes and produce the same goods and same results. Or so we were told.

We wrote the cheque. We ran down or disposed of stock. Monday morning came, and only about half the new versions of our standard products turned up, and half of them didn't work as promised. We had to go back to the nasty chemicals a few weeks in, and faced a considerable financial loss.

Now, everyone is determined to run their businesses sustainability. Suppliers are better informed, better geared, but it is still nowhere near as simple as it sounds, even if you are hugely knowledgeable.

A food success story

Paul Brown is the founder of BOL foods. After his hopes of either a professional rugby or a snowboarding career had been dashed, Paul says he found a true calling in a fridge in California: a fridge bursting with fresh, vibrant produce and delicious, healthy food in combinations he had never come across. All the food evolved around plants.

Inspired, Paul returned to the UK and worked for many years for Innocent. However, following Innocent's acquisition by Coca-Cola in 2015, it soon became apparent they would be refocusing its efforts on drinks. So, with both Innocent and Coca-Cola's blessing, Paul obtained backing from Innocent's founders (Jamjar Investments) to launch BOL in 2015. The brand initially launched with a healthy, fresh ready-to-go pot range, with the mission to help busy people eat well.

By the end of 2016, they had a £6m run rate and had just won Best New Business of the Year at the National Business Awards. They donated all their profits to Action Against Hunger and succeeded in their mission. But 52% of their original range included some meat or dairy ingredient, and the closer Paul came to the processes, the more uncomfortable he became with the impact this was having on the environment.

Paul watched Cowspiracy, read lots of books on the subject, and became aware of the Western diet's impact on people and the planet. He heard shocking statistics about the industrialization of our food system; for example, Paul says, that just a single beef burger requires 660 gallons of water and 18% of all global emissions come from animal agricultural production, which is more than the total produced by every method of transport combined.

Choosing what we eat is the single most significant environmental decision we make every day. Paul felt he had to think about the impact of this decision and how they wanted to grow the business. He decided to become part of the solution instead of the problem by removing meat, fish, and dairy from the range, thus going 100% plant-based. To highlight their resolves and values, they added a new mission: 'to help inspire the world to eat more plants'.

The decision brought enormous challenges; business halved overnight, and there was a point when Paul was not sure the company would survive. He remembers how difficult it was to tell the team to get their CVs ready, just in case. They spent much of that year in the kitchen developing new recipes and coming up with new ideas, and thanks to three sets of stakeholders, they came back stronger than ever.

Firstly, his team was more motivated and inspired than ever. Secondly, he credits his great investors, who are committed to the long-term future of BOL. Paul was initially nervous about breaking the news about the effect of his decision on sales. However, all his investors supported him, and since then, they have taken on more backers who join them in wanting to make a business to be proud of in the long run.

Third was the support from their customer partners. Telling some of the UK's biggest retailers that they were going to stop producing their bestselling recipes was a daunting prospect. But the retailers bought into the vision.

Paul says that it was a challenging process to go through, but he would go through it again in a heartbeat in order to lead a business delivering such a force for good. Success came from vision and values that all the stakeholders bought into.

A founder's challenge – working towards responsibility

So many of us start, as I did, with good intent, but little or no knowledge of what we can do to achieve sustainability. I turned to expert Tom Mills for some advice.

When he finished his Masters in Social and Political Science at Oxford, Tom took a job in the mining industry in Zimbabwe, believing he knew a great deal about what living on a mining site was like. Tom says that as he bounced his motorbike across the red earth, trying to navigate around potholed tracks and puddles that were often thigh-deep after the rains, he discovered that he could not have been more naïve.

He slowly came to understand that while he had believed he understood the complexities of African economies, he slowly learned that the system had its own way of functioning. What was truly the most 'sustainable' course of action at the mines was not what he had initially imagined. At that point, no measurement existed that could highlight the impact of these sorts of projects in a real, tangible, and comparable way.

In Afghanistan (where Tom worked as an advisor in the Ministry of Mines and Energy), Tom found another challenge. Over and above the economics of deals, there would be a barrage of ministerial questions. "What does this mean for my constituents to keep up with their neighbours? How are you valuing the development of skills this project will bring? How does this model illustrate the fair distribution of jobs? How have you valued the impact on our beautiful environment?" Answers were not to be found in desk-based research.

Tom has since led teams across the world for Banks and award-winning ESG investors on sustainability in natural resources and energy. He finds that business leaders and governments around the world today use words, phrases, and anagrams to talk about "responsibility" and "sustainability", but the truth is that the problem of ensuring business activity is sustainable is incredibly complex, and we are just at the nascent stage of measuring and valuing it.

He became convinced that we need better tools to measure and report impact effectively in the context of unique ecosystems and those who inhabit them. Tom founded Two Oceans Strategy to help businesses understand sustainability, measure their performance, and strategize a better future. He argues that while start-ups are built around solving urgent problems, there is no more pressing problem than the temperature of the planet and its impact on the lives of all of us who inhabit it.

The founders' challenge is measurement of what is sustainable, because that is what converts intention into impact. We have measured financial transaction for decades yet not developed ways of measuring the impact of our actions on our planet. Tom believes that a true understanding of what is sustainable only comes from being on the ground alongside those who will benefit from the processes, tech, or products you might be developing.

Tom shared the following recipe for sustainability and understanding the impact you can have and apply in your business:

1. Use leading sustainability frameworks, such as the Global Reporting Initiative, to understand what social, environmental and economic impacts are considered material in your industry. In other words, understand the most significant potential impact of your business.

2. Identify and create easy compilation methods for the data your business needs to produce the meaningful outputs defined by sustainability in line with those frameworks. You can do this by using the right technology and tools to help you do this in the most granular, affordable and efficient way, just as you would for your finances.

3. Compare your impact against that of your peers and identify hotspots where you can improve.

4. Set long, mid and short-term targets for non-financial outputs such as circularity, water usage, or carbon intensity.

5. Develop actionable road maps to take the appropriate steps to ensure that as your business grows, you have the right measures in place to create the best impact. For example, use software tools that can run scenarios to visualize how changes you make could impact those hotspots.

Strong Footings

etting clear on why you are doing what you are doing, what you believe in, and where you want to go, is crucial. If you haven't done it already, do it now.

But we can dream of all these things and still not start. The reason for this is usually fear, so we are going to look at what causes that fear to kick in when we think about starting a business, and how to overcome it.

There are a range of other things best thought of early to ensure you build on strong foundations. For example, there are the merits of having co-founders to consider, in particular, the warning "marry in haste and repent at leisure."

More and more start-ups are forming flat structures or considerably less hierarchical businesses. We look at successes past and present, why they worked or why they didn't.

Finally, it is all too easy to overlook your own relevance to successful growth. Growth is a roller coaster of a journey that both you and your business will be going on. You need support, to learn and grow to become your best self... to learn to be a leader. At the same time, you need to hone your business skills. I have chatted with people who have gone through this journey to find out what the benefits are of incubators and accelerators, and if business coaches or consultants are really worth the money when starting out...

CHAPTER SIX

Fear and Focus

W hat stops us from doing anything in life? Almost always, it is fear. Horrible, shaking, gut-clenching terror, or the sneaky kind that keeps you procrastinating and finding reasons why you will look again at doing something tomorrow. Remember that great George Addair quote, "Everything you've ever wanted is on the other side of fear"?

All that fear can cause you to seize up when it comes to starting and growing a business, or battling through tough times. Fear can paralyze us, cause our brains to fog, and leave us unable to think clearly, let alone make decisions. We argue ourselves out of doing things, and those things include starting a business. Yet right now, during these challenging, fearful times, if we re-frame our thinking, we might be able to see that it is also a time of incredible opportunities. So, let's look at fear and see if we can reduce its impact.

The first thing to do is to recognize it. The first sign is usually prevaricating. You start questioning if you have done enough research, or if you have chosen the right business name, or if this month is the correct month to plan to start. Perhaps next month would be better as you have your other half's birthday to plan... This sort of prevarication is the brain playing games with you, finding ways to avoid even looking at what you are afraid of.

Another reason why entrepreneurs battle with fear so much is that by nature, we want to achieve "more" and aim higher, so we have a natural tendency towards perfectionism. And perfectionism in business – or anywhere else – is an imperfect goal that piles on the pressure and causes more fear. Our self-confidence may not be that great either for various reasons we will look at later.

When I was struggling with fearfulness in recent years, someone I trusted kept saying to me, "Whatever it is that happens, you can cope with it". It took me some months and some other reading to unpick what this advice was really about. We can, and do, cope with what life throws at us. Often, a situation turns out not to be as bad as we first feared. What we are frightened of is not the thing itself (a business failing, a huge great spider, a plane ride). What really frightens us is that we won't be able to cope with it. You can cope with business success (and failure), so take a breath and go for it.

The Paradoxical Thinking about People who Fail

There is a terrible stigma about failure, especially in the UK, that makes us scared to put our heads up over the parapet. Entrepreneurs who deserve second chances have often been denied them as a result. Yet our feelings are paradoxical.

We also love a good "against the odds" story. We love to hear how KFC's fried chicken recipe was rejected over a thousand times, or how Walt Disney was fired from his first job because "he had no good ideas", how his first business failed and his funding applications for Disney World were rejected over three hundred times. Or how Brian Chesky and Joe Gebbia came up with the idea for Airbnb because they were so broke that they had to lease out their own apartment to pay the rent. Seven major investment companies turned them down before getting a break from Y Combinator.

US entrepreneurs, especially those in Silicon Valley, understand that there is no more excellent teacher than failure. In my last book, Scale for Success, Stephen Kelly describes how he nearly didn't get offered a job in Silicon Valley because he hadn't failed, a concept that might sound crazy in the UK. But the Valley's success has often been attributed to a combination of its access to talent and its level of forgiveness of failure. Most of the CEOs there have already failed, and that experience is highly valued. There is no greater teacher. Failure has its plus side.

Is the Reality of Failing that Unpleasant?

Of course, none of us like to fail. However, if you want to be an entrepreneur, you will discover that you fail on a virtually daily basis. But when we let that fear of failure take over, the only person who suffers is us. It is no different from a relationship you won't risk for fear of getting hurt. To succeed in business, you have to leap in and embrace those continual failures along the way. It won't be as bad as you think.

Rune Sovndahl, a Danish entrepreneur and co-founder of the globally successful Fantastic Services told me a story that demonstrates this so well. Rune says that he expected ups and downs in life, but he never expected to fail at things. One of his personal goals was cave diving. So, he set the scene perfectly, planned it all, rented the gear, and did cave diving courses. He was confident that he "had got this," especially having seen how unprepared the rest of his class were.

So, Rune was absolutely stunned when his instructor failed him at the last practical exam. In retrospect, Rune says the instructor was right to do so, and he went on to fail several more times. But the extraordinary thing was that Rune says he enjoyed failing. It was a new sensation, and he discovered that being challenged at levels he had never known existed made him appreciate the experience all the more and relish the chance of improving.

Rune says that he now realizes this is much the same in the business world, especially in the beginning when you will indeed fall, and yet get back up numerous times. He says that what is important is what you take away. If you have made a mistake, then learn from it; get up and grow. These failures will help you to realize where your abilities can get you and so they can teach you how to push beyond that, outside your comfort zone. Then, Rune advises, get an honest opinion from the best in your field and listen, improve, and achieve. Rune strongly believes failing is the only way to that sweet success.

Focus to keep your Mind off Failure

I remember chatting to English entrepreneur, Wilfred Emmanuel Jones. Wilfred made himself a promise as a child, growing up in the heart of Peaky Blinders Birmingham, that one day he would own a farm. He was written off at school, dishonourably discharged from the army, yet his dream never wavered. It would take him decades, but he finally bought his farm in rural Somerset.

When he launched The Black Farmer brand, it was tough to get off the ground. People told him the name would never work. The supermarkets wouldn't stock him. Wilfred had to re-finance his home as the banks wouldn't back him. Yet now he has one of the best-known food brands in the UK.

Wilfred had learned from his father that the way to succeed is to focus and have ruthless determination. He believes that passion is the only antidote to fear. When people tell him that they are scared to start a business, he tells them that "it is a lot like falling in love. People stop themselves because they are afraid of what might happen. Sometimes you do it despite everyone telling you that you are mad or making a huge mistake. You have to be consumed by it, not think of anything else. Like all great love affairs, it has its ups and downs, and part of the understanding of business is knowing that."

To turn your concept of failing on its head, Wilfred advises that an excellent measurement of life is to look back over the last year and think of the list of mistakes you have made. If you have a good list, you will have been living life to the full. I urge you to try it!

Passion does indeed carry you past fear, and through many trials and tribulations. So never, ever, not for the tiniest moment, lose sight of why you are doing what you do.

What I have learned to combat fear

Fear seems to get worse with age! Here are some of practical steps you can take that help.

First, recognize and avoid people who tell you that "you can't do it" or "you are wasting your time." Listen out for them and steer clear of them.

We have to also be careful of repeating negative things to ourselves. When we say we are "no good" or "haven't a hope," we may think it is modest, but we quickly start to believe it. Instead, try keeping a journal with your weekly wins, then look back and add up every deposit you've made into your confidence bank every month. Looking back will surprise you.

Many, many entrepreneurs battle with imposter syndrome. I remember the first thing I ever won in business was some free coaching. I was terrified. Six sessions were to be delivered by A Very Impressive Person, with an entire alphabet of letters after their name. They would, I was sure, only have to be in my office for five minutes to expose that any success I had ever had was, at best, just outrageous good luck. Years afterward, I heard about Imposter Syndrome for the first time and realized that my shaking terror had been a classic case.

Success does nothing to dispel the fear of failure – if anything it makes it worse. But what will see you through these challenges is a passion for what you are doing, a total focus on the desired outcomes, an increased recognition that the world doesn't end when you mess up, and the ability to re-frame failure as the best possible learning opportunity.

So, start your business, grow your business – surge ahead. You have nothing to fear in failure. Make fear, your new best friend.

CHAPTER SEVEN

Co-founders or Flying Solo

S tarting solo may well mean starting completely on your own, with no team at all in the very early days. Many entrepreneurs start that way briefly but it can be a hugely daunting prospect. There are many advantages of being part of a founding team, but making that decision has to be right for you. There is no one-size-fits-all answer.

Starting Solo

Many entrepreneurs do start on their own. I started several businesses like this, and I got to know the problems that people who start in this way have to face. There is a real issue over wearing a multitude of hats when it comes to customers. You tend to be passionate about what you do; your customers' happiness is of genuinely huge importance, and that combination can make it easy for you to sell authentically.

However, it is a nightmare when you are debt collecting. There you are on the phone, building the relationship, joyfully making a further sale, and then you have to switch to ultimatum mode, telling them if they don't pay, they won't get further supply. Alternatively, you go too soft on the credit control and end up not being paid.

One trick is to realise that you do not always have to reveal who you are – the boss – when you pick up the phone. Customers keep you chatting, and so do sales people. Till you have a team to protect you, one answer is to have an alter-ego, an invented side-kick who works for you. This is a ruse I used continually when debt collecting, and it made life a lot easier. Far from just pretending not to be you, this is about creating a whole new persona, with an email address, a style of writing, font and a personality you recognize. It really helps.

One massive plus if you start on your own is that you continue to own the whole business, but this fact won't make the loneliness of being responsible for everything go away. And you may have to create an alter-ego to answer your phones or collect payments, or indeed for any job you need to distance yourself from.

Starting with Co-founders – the downside

Starting with co-founders is becoming more and more popular, not least because investors often encourage it. One issue is that many partnerships are between husbands and wives. With a divorce rate of 40.91% in the UK and 44.62 % in the US[1], it is easy to see where that can create problems for businesses. I was jointly running a business when my ex and I parted early on. I will never forget our accountants assuring me that very few companies survive their co-owners divorcing, due to both costs involved, and split focus.

It is sadly true that co-founder disputes are one of the biggest reasons that start-ups fail. That statistic cannot be ignored. Also, like any close relationship, when it turns sour, it can turn vicious.

---

1   https://en.wikipedia.org/wiki/Divorce_demography

Mitigating the Risk with Co-founders

Like any relationship, when things are thriving, everything is wonderful. There is little time to dwell on irritations or even deep-seated disagreements. But when work levels go quieter, these all tend to surface. There can also be resentment if one of you is more passionate, harder working or more committed than the other.

A co-founders' agreement, with clearly set out roles and responsibilities, will help mitigate the damage but not eradicate it completely. Even informally dividing up business responsibilities will help – especially if it plays to your individual strengths – as you can begin to focus on the outcomes that each person achieves.

As with any relationship, a successful partnership will depend on how adept you both are at handling conflict. Even good friends fall out in business because the parameters of business and friendship are very different. Buried disagreements are fatal, but then so are ongoing, day-in-day-out screaming rows. A good start is to agree on no-go areas in heated discussions (name-calling, personal insults, throwing things). People who naturally run from conflict will have to do some work on themselves. You need to stay in the room and work out disagreements rather than take the fastest route out the door. Being a pushover isn't healthy, but neither is being the local bulldozer.

Risk Mitigation

One company that used to supply a business of mine was run by a pair of artisans who had been best friends from childhood. Imagine Tweedledum and Tweedledee, doing everything together. Naturally, the business was set up on an equal partnership agreement.

Everything was going well until both, in quick succession, got married. The wives hated each other on sight, and the friendship turned toxic. That would have been bad enough. However, the stronger character of the two decided that he wanted the business for himself. The leverage was straightforward but devastating. He stayed at home, drawing half of the profits, and continued to do so till his partner eventually walked way. It broke both the friendship and the business.

Bhairav Patel is Managing Director of Atom CTO, who provide tech advise to SMEs. During his career, Bhairav had experience in big corporations including IBM and PwC, small start-ups, and several global financial technology companies (Fintechs). As start-up advisors, they see many mistakes being made by founders starting out. The primary one is that they hire their mates as co-founders and give too much equity away, only to find out that their co-founders aren't pulling their weight. They then have to work out how to get rid of them.

Bhairav has also seen many instances where a co-founder is brought on board early on, doesn't do what they said they would do, yet walks away with 25% of the company because the original founder didn't have good/bad leaver clauses in their shareholder agreements. One of the worst examples of this was a married couple who had founded a moderately successful business. The wife persuaded her husband to bring in a third person as a co-founder and give him a healthy portion of shares. The husband found out later that his wife and the new co-founder had been having an affair. He lost his marriage and the company to them. Bhairav advises that when you are giving shares to someone working within the company, you tie those shares to responsibilities that they need to perform and that you vest those shares over a period of time. In addition, always make sure that your contracts are tight and that you have the ability to take shares from non-performers.

In favour of co-founders

Given these dangers, what are the plusses that make having co-founders an increasingly popular option? One reason is, of course, shared start-up costs or extra capital. It can also make raising investment easier as investors prefer teams, viewing them as safer bets, more solid and more proven, perhaps due to the greater range of expertise that a team provides.

Some accelerators only accept teams and others will automatically group you with prospective co-founders you have never met before, test out all your business ideas, and have the group go with the strongest business concept. The principle is simple; the strongest team has the greatest chance of success. It is undoubtedly less lonely, and you have people alongside you to share the highs and the lows of the journey.

Then there is the benefit of different perspectives. For example, someone from a different background or age group will often see a different aspect of something to you. They will also have different skill sets, and a well-balanced team means each co-founder can concentrate on what they do best and enjoy the most. Each will bring a different set of contacts, and a great network may be crucial to your business's growth.

Only a co-founder will understand every nuance of the business and have the same desire as you do to protect the investment you have both made. For example, you can pick each other up when one of you hits a brick wall or for whatever reason aren't able to work.

It is paramount to establish if there is enough common ground to make for a workable future, and, crucially, to explore each other's values thoroughly. Values are, of course, individual, but if something that your prospective partner feels is unimportant, is vital to you, it should be a massive red flag. It is essential to be compatible on those core values, because in future, you will be building every decision on top of them.

Test out some of these by exploring the choices ahead, setting out key milestones you want to achieve, finding out what success means to each of you, and see if you are on the same page. You can also compare how you would handle the problems that will come up, from demanding customers to cash-flow crises. Find out what their non-negotiable areas are. Ensure you unearth how important ego and standing are to both of you, as that can be a real issue if there is a fundamental clash of personalities.

Skill sets are easier to see and match together, and identical strengths add nothing to a team. Try drawing up an ideal co-founder skill set as you would for any other position, highlighting honestly to yourself where your greatest weaknesses lie. It might feel safe to bring in someone similar, or a friend, but that isn't always a wise decision.

Instead, use networks, forums, industry groups and social media groups, as you might for any other senior position. Take your time. And always remember that it would be better to go it alone, surrounded by brilliant experts and advisors than rush to commit to the wrong co-founder.

CHAPTER EIGHT

Alternative Business Structures

C ompany organizational structure is something you want to think about early, ideally before you start hiring, as structures are hard to "unpick" later on. For example, hiring traditional right hand and left hands, and then deciding further down the road you want to run a flatter structure will probably not go down well.

Hierarchal structures are pyramid-shaped, so they carry one or more layers of middle management and are the traditional corporate structure. Many coaches, HR companies, and undoubtedly Health and Safety companies want the clear job descriptions, job titles and clearly allocated responsibilities that come with the traditional hierarchies. But for many founders, running a hierarchy-based company may not have much appeal, especially if you have been part of a toxic hierarchy in the past.

Flat organizational structures, the polar opposite, are sometimes confused with co-operatives owned and operated by the people who use their products or services. The latter will still have a management structure in place. Flat structured companies are an alternative way of achieving a self-managing organization. The concept appears utopian, creating workplaces where everyone can do what they want, and work on projects. they choose.

There are different approaches and different degrees of flatness. For example, in some, employees are grouped according to function, enabling the teams and groups they form to be more independent, bypass middle management and report to higher levels. Another flatter structure is known as a matrix, where several divisions are divided into subsidiaries, increasing transparency and minimizing layers of bureaucratic management.

Holacracy

Holacracy is one of the best-known examples of flat structures. Developed in 2007, its aim was to ensure people are happy and productive in order to help companies reach their goals. Pyramid organizations are replaced by self-managed teams, de-centralizing management and organizational governance.

Ambiguities are removed to ensure transparency. Roles replace job descriptions, and employees are allocated to circles. Within the circles will be "energisers" to bring the necessary dynamism to the group. As opposed to managers making decisions, people who do the work are part of the decision-making process. This structure allows people to develop their potential but needs high personal accountability.

The purpose and the "why" of a company are always at the heart of everything that is done. However, the individual can do their role how they want, providing it doesn't interfere with anyone else and is in line with both that role and its goal. If that all sounds chaotic, it may be surprising to know that not only does structure still exist, but some people find it extreme.

Several well-known companies adopted it from those early years and their converts are outspoken in their conviction. This new structure didn't suit everyone. Team members, too, were often mixed in their reactions. Some companies walked away, citing that the structured nature needed was not what they were looking for. Others stuck with it, evolving their own variations to make the new concept work for them.

A Success Story

Danny Matthews is the owner of a branding and design studio, and developed his own organizational style, having read of the work of Cali Ressler and Jody Thompson, authors of "Why Work Sucks and How to Fix it." Ressler and Thompson carried out an experiment at Best Buy, introducing a results-based workplace. During this study, everyone was able to work whenever they wanted and how they wanted, providing the work got done.

Danny had worked in a traditional firm and watched people being rewarded for the hours they worked, while what they achieved was ignored. Promotions went to the people who logged in first in the morning, not the people who recorded the highest achievement figures.

Danny was determined to do things differently and used "the Saturday question" to help understand and explain what they were aiming at. On Saturdays, we humans all rush around getting what we need to do done so that the rest of the weekend is our own, to sleep, play football, see a movie, or whatever else takes our fancy. Danny believes every day should look like this and therefore it is entirely acceptable for anyone to go shopping, sleep, or watch daytime TV... provided the work gets done well.

Danny and his team drew up 12 principles, some from the Best Buy scheme and some of their own invention, which included the abolition of work schedules and the banning of any mention of how many hours, or how late you have worked.

He found people struggled to get their heads around it at first. People and businesses have been conditioned to judge each other by time spent working since the concept of 9-5 was first introduced with industrialization. When one illustrator joined them, they sent Danny a nervous message on Slack saying, "going into town to buy some new shoes but will be back at 2 pm". Dan wrote back and said, "excited for you about the shoes; send photos. Work wise, I don't need to know about this. Have fun!"

The downside is that people accustomed to being judged solely on the number of hours they work have lost some of their ability to take responsibility for themselves along the way, and Danny finds it can be hard to convert them back. Overall, however, Danny is finding it a great way to work and he hopes that his team will be ambassadors of a new way of doing things when they move on to other companies in the future.

Substituting Partners for Employees

Another way to grow without expanding your directly managed team is through partnerships. You can do this in the same way as large corporations set up separately operating subsidiaries that retain specific common brand characteristics. You can grow a multi-national company with this method.

I first learned of how this can be approached from an entrepreneur called Roger Jackson, who applied it to his market research company, Shopper Intelligence. Roger has partners in every country rather than employees. Overall, the partners are driven by the same outcomes. Each country may have slightly different ways of working, so flexibility and patience are key, but this system is not about creating identical franchises but about encouraging individuality in each partner to develop their business area. Instead of friction, it results in the relationships between them becoming less transitionary, much more fun, and more personal, making working a pleasure. Roger is free to work on the business, not in it, and the size of their reach gives them credibility with large clients that they would never have individually managed.

It is well worth some consideration.

Is there a Perfect Answer?

I have spoken to other companies that have adopted less hierarchical organizational structures of some sort, and all have had to work hard at them, adopting parts of the principles and dropping others. Three aspects particularly stand out.

The amount of time managers spend in communication increases dramatically. Otherwise, people or teams can float around without focus. The second is that some people are uncomfortable working in this sort of structure, which relies on people being transparent and accountable – something that not everyone finds natural. Motivation can also be a problem, as there is no clear career path for moving up. Finally, the larger the scale, the more unwieldy these structures become.

There is, of course, no silver bullet with any structure. But more and more companies are experimenting with putting together a less hierarchal approach than was common in the old days 'down the mill' and many have found greater employee empowerment and satisfaction, quicker decision-making processes, and lower labour costs without layers of middle management even if not committing to a completely flat structure.

Start-ups tend to be holistic by nature, with everyone highly involved, everyone knowing what needs doing, and often everyone able to jump in and do anything required in the beginning. Structural problems can strike a mortal blow at the growth stage, and the further you plan in advance and recruit people who suit that structure and are committed to making it work, the more chance it has of succeeding.

CHAPTER NINE

The Power of Networking

The American motivation coach Jim Rohn is accredited with saying that you are the average of the five people you spend the most time with. Studies show that these averages can extend to a broader group of your friends and acquaintances, and that they can affect not just your knowledge levels, but your mental and physical health as well.

Small wonder, therefore, that the negative impact of the company you keep can knock you sideways. To what extent can you remain positive surrounded by people who tell you that you can't make it, or how far will you progress in a group of people whose interest in stretching their brain is considerably less flexible than their underwear elastic.

Some people advise you to audit the people you spend time with. I don't think that is worth doing continually, but it is certainly a worthwhile exercise to carry out occasionally. Ask yourself who energizes you, whom you are learning from, and whom you spend most of your time with. That analysis could teach you a great deal about where you pick up negativity, and make it clear what and who truly helps you to develop.

When you start and grow a business, most of your time and energy is absorbed into that process. There is often barely any time for family, let alone for old friends. Yet networking is considered part of business life, and it may be essential for sales if your market is local businesses or specific sectors.

Networking on familiar turf, however, will rarely progress you as a person, and it may even prevent you from developing not just *your* full potential, but that of your businesses, too.

Networking with purpose

With networking, you need to be very clear on your goals. If it is necessary to go and find customers on a local level, for example, consider it part of your sales job or delegate it to whoever is in charge of sales.

If you want to grow yourself and your business fast, you will need to find a group of fast-growth entrepreneurs. It will not matter if you are the smallest or the least knowledgeable. That can even be a good thing, as it will stretch you to the maximum.

Some people deliberately cultivate the rich, the famous, the useful. The downside to this is that these people are more than accustomed to being surrounded by people who want things. Therefore, if any relationship develops, it will tend to remain mostly superficial. It is far better to cultivate a circle of people who will develop you as a human being...

Networking for Development

Truly successful entrepreneurs go out of their way to cultivate relationships with people who are more knowledgeable than them. Even extremely busy and successful entrepreneurs will usually answer a specific and politely put question if approached with respect for them and their time. You can go one step further by making it part of your personal development plan.

I had the great pleasure of interviewing the American entre-preneur and global expert in 3D and machine learning, Richard Boyd (of Tanjo.ai). Richard told me how even at college, he would go out of his way to buy a coffee for the smartest people he could possibly find in any field that interested him. It was an entirely deliberate policy of self-development.

Richard began his career selling mobile phones, and accelerated its development through this policy of relentless learning. He worked with directors like James Cameron and Sydney Pollack and created computer game companies with Tom Clancy, Michael Crichton and Ozzy Osbourne. He demoed software to Bill Gates, Scott Cook, Larry Ellis and Steve Wozniak, and did a software deal with Kevin O'Leary.

By the time one of his companies, 3Dsolve, needed financing, he and the group he worked with were able to consider who they knew in Silicon Valley. One contact led to Reid Hoffman, who had just left PayPal along with Elon Musk and Peter Thiel. Richard had also met Joi Ito in Japan when he was still a DJ, a long time before Joi became the director of the MIT Media Lab, and both Reid and Joi invested in 3Dsolve. Recently, Richard says he saw an article entitled "The eight people who secretly run the world." Joi and Reid were two of them:

The scope from learning from others is limitless if you are careful about the people you choose to learn from. Business schools teach a bundle of very beneficial processes and procedures, but these tools will only take you so far. It is when you are running your business that the learning really starts. People on the same journey will help... and those further along will help even more.

The day you stop learning is the day your business stagnates. Learning has become even more necessary with the acceleration of tech during the pandemic. Software companies are changing so fast now that it is hard even for experts to keep up. The same is true of AI and machine learning, and if you don't progress, you and your business will quickly become irrelevant. But it isn't just the practical things you need to keep learning. To grow a business successfully, you have to become an excellent leader, and becoming an excellent leader means continually working at becoming the best version of you. That has to be your priority.

Networking to change your reality

Should you still have doubts about the power of networking, let me tell you the extraordinary story of Andrey Yashunsky. Andrey grew up in Israel and became an Air Marshall for the second half of his twenties. His identity had to remain hidden behind a plausible cover story.

The story they came up with was this; that he owned a company named Prytek, which was raising capital for Israeli technology ventures. He was tasked with building relationships and, by the age of 26, had a more extensive network than a professional Wall Street Banker. Many of those contacts came from travelling in business class on flights between major cities such as New York, London, and Beijing. Andrey says that this helped him build access to the wallets of HNWI (high net worth individuals), which he would later introduce to Israeli start-ups.

By the age of 27, he had already closed ten genuine deals raising capital from NHWI for Israeli start-ups. By 28, he had access to unique under-the-radar Israeli technology start-ups and also what he describes as billion-dollar wallet connections. Israeli start-ups were looking for capital, and rich people were looking for opportunities. His real job as an Air Marshal was just a connecting base, but nobody cared what else he did as long as he delivered.

Andrey decided he needed to get into a fund or an investment banking position, so he used his network to support him with credential letters. He moved to London, and after only a month at a mid-ranking firm, he had acquired a position within a UK investment bank. From there, Andrey achieved a position as Vice President in Russia's top business bank, responsible for raising investment for a mezzanine fund. Within six months, he was originating his own deals, and within a year, he was able to quit the Vice President position to open his own fund, again supported by his network. Andrey is now the founder and CEO of the company named, of course, Prytek. Prytek focuses on building businesses and ecosystems in the Financial Services, Cyber, Tech, Education and HR sectors.

CHAPTER TEN

Mentors, Coaches, and Consultants

Entrepreneurial groups can be excellent sources of learning, as can incubators and accelerators and other entrepreneurial courses. As the business grows and morphs out of the initial start-up stage, they all help can help you to develop and start to step back from and out of the company, as per the well-known Michael Gerber quote, "work on your business, not in it."

The people you meet there are also invaluable for many different reasons, not least because running a business is an incredibly lonely job. Other founders understand the challenges better than anyone and will be there to brainstorm, support, and re-rail you.

A mentor can also be an important addition to your journey. A mentor can be someone who changes your life and takes you to a new level. Several mentors are even better - it is now quite common to seek out specialist mentors for different areas of your life and business to maximize your potential and growth. Remember that any mentor will have a skill set in one area but may not be brilliant at other things, so stay on subject. Good mentors help you develop your potential with a combination of believing in you and kicking you as needed, and I rarely hear negative stories surrounding mentors.

Then there are consultants and business advisors and unfortunately horror stories about them abound and the following is just one example.

Advisors that take years to recover from

Dr Wei-Shin Lai was a family physician who struggled to get back to sleep when patients rang her on the nights she was on duty. She tried meditational music, but the headphones involved were bulky and smaller earbuds were uncomfortable. Dr Lai and her husband, Jason Wolfe, made their own; Jason soldering while she sewed together five hundred of what would become their SleepPhones®, to offer to her patients. The SleepPhones®, worked so well that the couple founded AcousticSheep LLC, a multi-award-winning business.

Dr Lai learned the hard way not to accept what all business "experts" say. One advisor pushed them to enter large mass-market stores with their niche product. They got rejection after rejection from buyers telling them the same thing: that their product was too niche. They knew that their products weren't for everyone and that they might not be ready to service the biggest chain stores. However, this advisor repeatedly told them to "not give up" – because this was where his products had found success in the seventies.

When they finally got an opportunity to look at a deal, they saw that the financials involved were high risk, but still their advisor ignored their concerns. Rather than helping them through the negotiations to optimize the transaction, he told them not to worry and to go ahead. It took them nearly three years to dig themselves out of a hole that, thanks to their advisor, could have ended their company.

Dr Lai has seen this repeatedly since her first experience with that advisor business leaders with a method that worked well for them in their sector when it was new, perhaps twenty years ago. Good advisors have to have relevant experience and listen to your concerns before advising you, but instead, all too often, they simply enjoy regaling you with glorious stories of their ancient successes rather than slog through the hard stuff with you. I too have heard many of these.

Business Coaches

People often confuse the role of a business coach with a business consultant (including, sadly, some of the people with those titles). Consultants should bring business expertise. Coaches should not offer advice but coach you to develop, help you identify goals, and hold you accountable for reaching them. Given that coaching is an unregulated industry and the amounts charged can be eye-watering, it is crucial to do a lot of research before putting your money down. Ask to speak to other people that have worked with any potential coach.

If you aren't moving nearer to reaching your potential, they are not the right coach for you. It is a very individual relationship, and you need to be pushed to new levels. However, there is a degree that the pushing shouldn't reach. I had monthly sessions with a very well renowned coach a long while ago. After a few months, I noticed myself getting severely tense and anxious in the lead-up to the sessions, feeling tearful the whole way through and emerging on the other side with zero confidence. It was, without question, a bad match. So, don't commit to anything long term; remember, what works for one person may not work for another.

Coaches also come with a buyer beware sign

Coaches can have a fantastic effect on your business, but a positive outcome is far from guaranteed. I suffered a succession of either unsuitable or just outright appalling ones. Sometimes there is an immediate gap in expectation that everyone should be aware of. The business owner may be green, lonely or stuck in a bad place. What attracts them to the idea of coaching in any of those cases is to make their situation better, make them safer, make the problems go away.

Someone who is desperately looking for a solution to an emotional situation is a gift for any salesperson; with very little persuasion, the desperate business owner hears the voice of re-assurance, safety and possibly even friendship being extended. It is very easy for them to get hooked: hooked on the initial sale and then on the sessions thereafter.

The sessions then increase. What may have started by zoom, becomes in person, which can mean a vast expenses bill for the coach's travel and accommodation. Despite the business being in trouble, the desperate entrepreneur goes on paying out more and more cash that they absolutely can't afford. It can take a long while and, unfortunately, a good dollop of unpleasantness for the entrepreneur to get wise and finally resolve to part company with their coach.

I have come across entrepreneurs acting as coaches or mentors looking for very desperate, emotional business owners. Members of this group are on the look-out for businesses to acquire on the cheap – in a completely unscrupulous and unethical way. Even some highly reputable coaches will have an arrangement whereby any client wanting to sell their company is offered an introduction to a specific VC, from which they collect a fee.

All these things happened to me over the years. Of course, there are success stories too. But it is an overcrowded and unmonitored industry with a lot of sharks out there, many of whom are business people with little or no training (or interest) in coaching. What they will have is a sales process that has been refined to offer the words of reassurance that you want to hear.

Never forget that coaching is a business transaction; it should be approached as such.

Successful Coaching

Jenni Field is the founder and director of Redefining Communications. In the beginning, the business was going well; she had a book deal with a publisher and a clear message for her audience. By the time the business was three years old, Jenni thought it was time to invest in herself and the company to enable it to grow even faster.

Having signed up with successful coach, Chris Ducker, Jenni has found it hugely beneficial. She was aware that one of the issues she struggled with was price, forever battling the voices in her head that worried that she was charging too much. Chris suggested a call to talk it through. On the call, they broke down what would be involved in each piece of work she was charging for and how long it would take. Jenni could immediately see in real terms that her pricing was fair and justified, and she never struggled again.

The next benefit was that coaching has helped her gain clarity on what is right for her business and not what other people say is right for it. Jenni says that we live in a world of comparison, and it is all too easy to get distracted by someone else's opinion.

She regularly tells herself to "keep on trucking" instead, and now that she has clarity, she can stay focused on reaching her goals. She also finds that the regular calls and knowing she will be kept accountable helps with that focus. Jenni's tip is that some people enjoy group coaching and others work better one to one. There are pros and cons to both, but it is crucial to find out which suits you best for coaching to be successful.

In the two years since she started being coached, Jenni has increased her business turnover by nearly 70%, written another book, and created a podcast. It has undoubtedly been successful. Jenni says that she initially debated getting either a non-executive director or a business coach, and thought that either would strengthen the business. Chris has been coaching her as a person. She knows that soon the company will need a non-exec to develop its progress as well. The two roles are very different.

Conclusions

From the moment you start your business, you will be besieged by offers of help and advice at varying cost and hugely varying quality. It is important to be clear in your own mind what the correct functions of mentors, advisors and coaches are, how relevant their experience is in delivering in that role, and what you are looking for them to deliver. Set those goals for a particular period, and if they don't work, move on.

That you will need to develop is a given, and the first step is to admit you need help – but the second is to pause and find the right person or people that you can really trust to guide you. The right people will help you develop in ways you might not have been able to achieve on your own.

Incubators and Accelerators

More and more entrepreneurs are opting to go through incubators and accelerators. These are often thought of in connection with funding, but there are many additional advantages, including providing you with a support system. There is a vast choice of them now, but as with any growth market, there can be huge variations in quality.

Here are three entrepreneurs' experiences, from university-based incubators to the prestigious Y Combinator in California, to help you decide if incubators and accelerators are the right choice for you – and how to select one that suits you best. Then the next hurdle is to be accepted...

Expectations, choices and diverse experiences

Shem Richards, the Australian entrepreneur behind the brilliant Goldilocks Suit, has experience of both incubators and accelerators. He suggests that you find one backed by people who have been there and done it themselves. He found that some are run by big corporations with no experience in starting or running a business. Others are run by someone fresh out of university.

Another piece of advice from Shem is to find somewhere that specializes in your field. The advisors will be smarter than you, and will also bring contacts within that field to listen, learn and develop from. When Shem went through an incubator that had a shared workspace, he found that its sector-specific nature meant that everyone had similar issues and could work on solutions together.

Shem cites peer learning as one of the greatest benefits of this arrangement. When the accelerators are held in person, cohorts go off and have tea together after a session. They might compare notes and experiences, talk about how one of them had pitched to a particular investor and what they were like, or discuss the merits of a consultant one of them had met that the others were considering working with. It was invaluable, saved a lot of time, and helped in the process of trying to identify the best VCs or consultants, where to find and target your customers or how to get to key opinion leaders. Shem says that those cups of tea accelerated their growth far more than the accelerator themselves, and that what he learned there paid for the accelerator.

Shem warns that it is easy to expect lots of attention and a flood of investors when you start winning pitch competitions. In reality, people only engage when you have traction. Until then, you need to do your own shouting. Now, six years in, they have people coming to them, but Shem learned to be incredibly noisy before that.

Shem also says that generosity is a big secret to success. Even now, busy as he is, he always tries to take ten minutes to help anyone who asks him a question. Without fail, it pays him back a hundredfold. When you have helped someone and later on ask them for an introduction or piece of advice, they will virtually always return the favour. That can be invaluable, not just in money, but in expertise and contacts.

The Ongoing Mentoring Benefit

Kalyan Gautham came from a small town in India. He was inspired by his grandfather's amazing tales of what he had achieved and the obstacles he had overcome. Today, Kalyan is the Founder and CEO of *WATT*, the world's first platform for virtual marches, political rallies and charity walks. Through *WATT*'s tech, someone can, for example, run "a Boston Marathon" while in the UK, raising money for the same cause.

Kalyan always planned to start a global business, and he and his co-founder knew they had a strong vision. They felt Singapore had a better start-up ecosystem than India. So, they applied to the Antler Accelerator there. The accelerator was founded by Harvard graduates and is very unique. They invest in founders rather than businesses and then put people together, some of them having joined the accelerator without a developed idea.

Kalyan had only been to Singapore as a tourist, and yet suddenly he was swept up in its fast-moving ecosystem. The accelerator was full of amazing people doing extraordinary things, a few of whom have since moved to the US to continue to develop their businesses, just as Kalyan eventually did.

Until that point, Kalyan was very mission-driven, but he and his co-founder had no business model and no concept of how they would make money out of the idea; they had only a vision of the impact they wanted to achieve. The accelerator focused on financial viability, which Kalyan says was the most critical advice that they could have received, and propelled them along the learning curve.

Singapore-based VC Mikael Krogh became his advisor and provided them with US connections. Kalyan chose to re-locate from California to Cape Girardeau, a small town in Missouri, to establish their operations. It was an unconventional move, especially for a tech start-up, but Kalyan says there are many hidden gems outside the perceived 'Mecca of start-ups', and Cape Girardeau is one such place. Labour costs are cheaper, and attrition is exceptionally low. They can recruit from the large university there and invest in upskilling. But more importantly, for a socially focused company, they are able to live their mission by helping the local ecosystem.

Support from the contacts in the accelerator continued in the US. After *WATT* launched, they went through a difficult time and nearly ran out of cash. They had an investment offer, but Kalyan knew the investors' values weren't a good fit, and they wanted a huge chunk of equity and a board seat with voting rights. Mikael Krogh steered them to re-think the business model, to pivot to ensure that it worked, and so enable the company to turn down the investment and thrive without it.

The Y Combinator experience

Andrew Barnes is co-founder of Go1, the hugely successful online learning platform. Initially, Andrew was studying in the UK; another friend was with the United Nations, one had graduated a computer science programme, while a fourth, Vu Tan, was studying medicine. Vu was finding that rotating through different programmes from different training providers meant he was constantly repeating hand-washing training because there were no coordinated records of achievement. It seemed a ridiculous waste of time, and Andrew and Vu had the idea of an online learning platform for training that coordinated qualifications.

They were starting to work out how to do it when Andrew woke up in the middle of the night with a brainwave and sent himself an email. He says this is a habit he has never broken, and most of the emails look crazy in the light of day. This one told him to urgently apply to Y Combinator. Andrew knew applications were closing that day, but when he got up and started filling everything in, he saw that the deadline was sooner than he thought due to the time change across continents. He managed to get hold of the other three and put something together in time.

If you are selected for Y Combinator, they fly you to California, all expenses paid. It should have been fantastic. Andrew arrived from England, desperately jet-lagged. Only two of the other three had been planning to come and had arrived the night before and gone for something cheap to eat. By the time they came to present, Andrew was keeling over from jet lag, and the other two had food poisoning. It made the whole presentation doubly challenging.

Despite everything, Andrew found that the experience bought many unexpected benefits. Almost immediately, they met the Airbnb founders, and other incredibly successful people came in to talk to them every week. Andrew admits he semi-expected to gain some silver-bullet success recipe. Instead, the message was to simplify their approach; that they had permission to focus on what they were doing and build something people love. That message was invaluable.

Choices

Accelerators and incubators may not choose you or you may not be a right fit for them. Only by going to see them, can you start to see what you might get out of your time there, how good a fit they might be. Funding might be part of it, and exposure might come in some small way, but it is the support from peers and mentors, along with the level of expertise and sheer brain power you are exposed to that really pays off:

CHAPTER TWELVE

Developing You

Starting a business is an exciting roller-coaster journey that will need you to change and develop in so many different ways. For example, there is a blurring of the lines now with so many founders calling themselves CEO (Chief Operating Officer) from day one, even though the roles of founder and CEO require very different skill sets. CEOs are more usually brought in for their experience to drive companies forward, while founders are the ideas people. If you are attempting to do both, you will need to learn even more.

As a CEO, you have to leave behind the practical skill you perhaps started your business with, the brilliant tech skills, or the superb teaching, and hand that work over to others on your team so that you can devote yourself to developing the business and to becoming a leader. To make space for development, you have to stop doing other people's jobs.

You will constantly need to invest the time to upskill. Big success stories Elon Musk, Mark Cuban, Mark Zuckerberg and Warren Buffet are all big readers. We have already talked about the value of networking, about coaches, peer groups, and specific high-growth clubs and programmes that can help in the effort to upskill. But while you need knowledge, you also need confidence. A CEO's job is to generate value for stakeholders and be the visionary that inspires everyone that comes into contact with the business: suppliers, customers, team, and investors too.

Time Blocking

With so much going on, it is hardly surprising that many entrepreneurs have turned to themed time-blocking. With themed time blocks, we don't dip into doing one thing, then check our social media, have a quick meeting, and finally check our social media again. Themed time blocks are set for longer periods and carefully planned the night before. They involve minimal, if any, social media. One theme, perhaps 'management', or 'customers' might last the whole day.

Time blocking is incredibly effective but it needs to be put in place with an awareness of other people and an equal respect for their time.

Physical health

This book isn't about giving you a health lecture. However, you cannot inspire others unless you value yourself, and believe that you are worth taking care of. Being at peak physical and mental health is part of performing well. The one single, irreplaceable asset that your business cannot do without... is you.

On a practical basis, there are the more obvious things such as staying hydrated, avoiding white processed carbohydrates, and exercising. Sleep can be a massive battle for overworked and stressed entrepreneurs, so healthy ways of solving that problem is crucial. Plan quality sleep as you would any other part of self-care. The less you sleep, the less productive you are. Self-care is as important for entrepreneurs as it is for their teams.

Go Bear Grylls and develop your mind

We talked of fear earlier and those unresolved terrors that often leave us with low confidence which then can result in poor decision making, affecting our whole lives, including our businesses. Most of us battle on regardless, which is self-defeating.

Mark Allen was living in North Queensland, Australia, with his wife, and they were juggling five small start-ups in both retail and hospitality. Mark had written in his blog about a horrible experience that still haunted him: being buried alive when a sand dune collapsed on him as a teenager. A production company putting together an episode of Bear Grylls' television show got in touch and suggested he fly to the Italian Alps to join Bear in a show where he takes people into extreme situations to make them face their fears.

They spent a week in the Italian Dolomites trekking through old battlefields from World War I. They would rest in turret encampments, and make their way through trenches that were still littered with barbed wire and tin cans discarded by the soldiers, lying in the freezing mountain air. The area was riddled with caves and tunnels dug into the Alps by hand-held chisels and pickaxes a century ago. Long skinny tunnels snaked around the mountain's edge, and sometimes opened up into vast, black caverns. They climbed down into one of these caverns and discovered that they couldn't get out the way they came; the only way to escape was to dig through the rubble of a previously caved-in exit. They managed to make a tiny opening by hand, and they needed to squeeze through one by one to find their way back into the sunlight.

At other times, they explored ice caves, some of which were pitch black. Mark could feel the walls closing in, and his shallow breaths starting to overwhelm him. The world was spinning, but Bear helped him face those fears and take emotion out of the situation so that he could operate effectively. With Bear's help and mental exercises, he sat in the caves and learned that it is sometimes the situation rather than the outcome that you are afraid of, and that this is what distracts you from being able to focus. Bear helped him to face the fear itself, and to face it head on. Bear would tell Mark, "Fear is an acronym for False Evidence Appearing Real - don't let your mind present false evidence that isn't real and make you upset. The ground you are standing on is solid; the walls of the cave have stood for over 100 years."

Mark found the experience incredibly helpful, especially in translating it back to business, where he became able to look at things with a more critical eye and take the emotion out of tough decisions. He could also determine what is real from what is false and make decisions without false emotion clouding his judgment, using evidence-based processes. Mark observes that when faced with decisions, we start worrying about what people will think, and all the different potential outcomes. The reality is that this is all false evidence.

Mark made tough choices, including closing two of his businesses and pivoting another. After his time with Bear, Mark could see that he could not control or worry about what people would think, and that the only real outcome that was his choice would be a closed business. With this new ability to make decisions and focus on what was important to deliver the best results, Mark was able to build up his remaining companies and sell them successfully.

He has since created a real-estate tech business, Patch. He used the same principles to win investment, working through a challenging hundred and seventy-two "nos" before finally securing investment from both international and Australian Venture Capital firms. He did not let himself focus on the fear of failure but rather on the reasons for not doing so, and kept going till he reached daylight.

Caution and self-awareness

We have to discover our own routes to self-development, but this discovery starts by being aware of certain entrepreneurial tendencies, not least that we believe will all be ok if we just keep working hard enough. The truth is that it is all too easy to burn out. Plus, if we believe we are of no value or try too hard to be the Nice Person, we forget to take care of ourselves – and both burn out and fail to have time for that crucial self-development.

In addition, research shows that while entrepreneurs are strong, hugely capable people on the outside, the inside often tells a different story. We are prone to behavioural addictions[1], of which being workaholics is one, but others often appeal too. A Berkeley study[2] found an incredible 72% of entrepreneurs to have a mental health difference, and a London-based specialist, Olivia James[3], also finds a high proportion to have had childhood traumas of some sort: financial, divorce, physical or emotional. The budding entrepreneur develops the habit of burying things, surviving, and believing they can cope. This is an incredibly useful habit in many ways, but it is also dangerous. We need to look after our own mental health and accept that entrepreneurs are also vulnerable and may need to ask for help.

It is a high-pressure journey, physically and mentally, but fun. Get the right support in every area so you can enjoy it.

---

1 https://www.entrepreneur.com/living/the-real-risk-of-entrepreneurial-strengths-becoming/283574

2 https://michaelafreemanmd.com/About%20Dr.%20Freeman.html

3 https://harleystreetcoach.com

Show Me
The Money

S tarting and growing a business takes both money for cash flow and money for capital outlay. Cash flow has some different options for funding so you can look at these separately or you may choose to try and raise money to cover both areas. Depending on the country that you're operating in, there can be attractive tax breaks for investors with the right gearing, such as the UK's Enterprise Investment Scheme. Each stage means larger amounts are required to be raised.

Investment has become a very complex business. There are Friends and Family funds, Early-Stage Funds, Government Funds, Regional Funds, International Investors, Crowdfunding options, individual investors and Angels, VCs, and VC companies.

Both angels and private investors are an excellent match for first-round (seed) investment or Series A funding. VC companies can be both large corporations or smaller groups of individual investors. These smaller groups of investors are successful individuals who work together and bring different strengths. These might be financial expertise, business acumen or access to a network, which, together, can add to the business and significantly improve its bottom line. There are also some very wealthy individuals that have FOs (Family Offices acting on their behalf) who invest up to £10m, and some of this cash does make its way to mid-range funding rounds.

Of course, in the early days at least, you could use a business model that pays its way, known as bootstrapping. Even now, do not forget that your way to success is to make money, and the quicker you do it, the better.

CHAPTER THIRTEEN

Bootstrapping

Recently, in an entrepreneurs' online group, someone asked for advice on start-up loans. They wanted to borrow a reasonably small amount for start-up costs and stock, and I suggested bootstrapping as an alternative. When I explained what that meant, they told me I was "obviously not someone who had ever run a business." Sadly, this said a lot more about their ignorance than mine – but it emphasizes how far we have strayed from the days when most businesses started by bootstrapped.

Funding Myths

Anyone who wants to understand the differences between financing in the US and UK can learn a lot from Stephen Halasnik. Stephen is Managing Director of US-based Financing Solutions and an entrepreneur who has founded several high-growth companies. He understands finance from both sides of the table and believes that negotiating your way through the world of finance is a rite of passage in entrepreneurship. If you use lack of finance as an excuse not to start a business, Stephen says, you haven't got what it takes to be an entrepreneur.

Finance is a problem that has so many possible solutions. Twenty-five years ago, there were only two or three potential sources. Now, there are so many more, yet Stephen also finds young entrepreneurs thinking they can only start with Angel or VC backing.

Stephen also suggests that one option is to start a small-scale business and re-invest the profits. You can begin at home. Then, if you are selling B to C (direct to consumers), you can ask for payment upfront. The margin you are charging should easily cover your credit card and cash flow. Stephen finds that the most common mistake is setting those margins too low margins and preventing there being any money over to re-invest for growth, which takes three years to get to at best.

Before the growth of tech businesses, it was virtually unheard of for any start-up to get financing as a complete start-up. Would-be entrepreneurs were heavily reliant on the undependable possibilities of bank loans, more often than not personally guaranteed against the family home.

The appearance of tech companies coincided with bank financing starting to dry up, and juicy scale-up deals became harder for investors to find. Some tech companies need to get to a certain size before becoming profitable and have had to sort out funding to achieve that. With potentially huge returns, investors moved into the start-up arena.

Massive funding is not essential

The reality is that even many of the tech giants started bootstrapped. Steve Jobs and Steve Wozniak began building computers in a garage, and Mark Zuckerberg wrote the first version of Facemash in his college. The GitHub founders kept their company bootstrapped throughout the six years it took till GitHub was ranked fourteenth on the Forbes Cloud 100 list.

Australian entrepreneur Matt Bullock spotted an opportunity for a secure payment gateway for credit payments. He wrote the code for the software, swapped a crate of beer for a logo design and a banner, then placed an ad in an internet magazine and found a customer. It wasn't a quick route to success. But by eighteen years in, Eway was processing payments for 36 billion dollars per annum, and Matt sold the company for seven times the value of its yearly revenue.

Mailchimp is another example. Founders Mark Armstrong, Dan Kurzius and Ben Chestnut ran a website design company and had inquiries for email marketing help. Ben put something together from some old code, and Mailchimp was born. The founders all agreed not to take on VC funding because they believed they could generate the revenue through the software itself – which, of course, they did.

Some entrepreneurs take out personal loans in order to bootstrap. Sara Blakely of Spanx is another famous example. Blakely remained the owner of the company, turning that initial loan of $5,000 into a personal worth of over a billion. Personal loans involve a lot of risk, and the pressure that they bring are not for everyone – but for those who can make them work, the rewards can be significant.

Bootstrapping – the pros, the cons and the how

Bootstrapping means surviving on minimal borrowing, perhaps just a little from family and friends, or funding through sales.

This approach results in a slower start, and very little (if any) income for the founder. But the pay-off means that you own the business outright for longer, or indeed for the long-term, and all the equity remains with you, as it did with Spanx's Sara Blakely. You also still control the company's ethos, so it remains true to your beliefs and values.

Recent data[1] showed that, in the US, angels fund 0.91% of start-ups, compared to the 0.05 % that are funded by VCs. In 2021 the Scale Up Institute was quoting a shortfall of £15bn[2] between the finance available and the finance needed by scaling companies. You may have to consider bootstrapping simply because your chances of successfully obtaining funding are low.

Bootstrapped companies should always show stronger balance sheets because they aren't put into the red with debt. If you don't have the option of funding, it does also teach you very tight fiscal control. Founders feel it is "their money" in an inevitably more personal way.

While growth may be slower, the arguments that it is impossible to hire staff or do any marketing, or that you will lose out on vital connections, are not entirely valid. You can work on your own as Matt Bullock did, work with equally invested partners, or inspire others to come in and work in return for equity in the company as another way of raising early funds. Marketing doesn't have to be expensive, especially with many inspiring guerrilla marketing campaigns finding success. You can, as discussed earlier, make building connections part of your deliberate self-development plan for the price of just a few coffees.

At the very start of my last business, I was penniless, with no resources and absolutely no hope of anyone lending me any money to start a business. It didn't stop me. I planned a business that suited my lack of resources; a selling operation that needed virtually no cash. My office consisted of a shelf under the stairs

---

1 https://www.entrepreneur.com/article/230011

2 https://www.growthbusiness.co.uk/50-of-britains-scaleups-expect-to-raise-finance-this-year-2559282/

at home, a second-hand fax phone, and a card index box. The big gamble was a very second-rate leaflet that I bought on the remaining room left on my credit card. It was the days before the internet, so every week when I got my social cheque (yes, I was that broke), I would buy some stamps and a trade phone directory. Then off into the post some leaflets would go. That sort of crazy approach was unheard of at the time. Anyone thinking of starting a business was pointed straight to their bank to take out a heavily-secured loan. But in retrospect, it was textbook bootstrapping.

This approach brings with it the advantage of focusing you on one crucial problem: getting a customer that will pay for what you do. This is, after all, the crucial test of any business: will people part with their hard-earned cash?

Getting help from your suppliers is riskier. Even further back in time, I started a sandwich business. Broke at the time, I arranged to get the ingredients on credit from the corner shop in the morning and pay them back out of sales in the afternoon. Slowly, I needed to put less "on tick" and spend more upfront. The time lag between my borrowing, being paid, and repaying was workable, at only a few hours. Had I persevered, it would have been perfectly possible to build the sales and therefore the revenue to the point of employing more people to sell, and so eventually move over to wholesalers. Depending on your business model, you may have to fund some or all of that gap between getting paid t and paying out.

The anonymous entrepreneur I mentioned at the start who so objected to the idea of bootstrapping was looking to get into a high-end goods market. Another suggestion I made was to start with something simpler, at a lower cost, and build up from there. He didn't like that idea either. Yet when you consider those huge, and eventually hugely-funded tech companies that have used the principle of an MVP as a kick-starter and early funding (more of MVP's later) you can see that humble beginnings do not stop true entrepreneurs.

CHAPTER FOURTEEN

Family, Friends, Factoring and Banks

I f you are selling something that costs you nothing, or you get paid immediately, you may not need a capital raise for the initial few weeks or months of your business. You may even raise some minimal funds from selling the contents of your attic – but pretty soon, you will be faced with the nitty gritty of cash flow issues. Borrowing for cash flow has some different possibilities to borrowing for capital, and family and friends can still be an option. There are also government loans and grants (depending on where you live and what sector you are in) that might help with start-up costs or cash flow.

Customer Payments for Cash Flow

Stephen Halasnik's first business was a product one and didn't need finance because his customers always paid him upfront. He became a great proponent of this business model, but it is often met with resistance. People worry about the impact that asking for money up front will have on their customers.

Stephen had a good friend with a large home-entertainment business supplying all the mega-stars. These were hundred-thousand-dollar systems, and Stephen's friend found the cash flow impossible. Stephen advised him to ask for 50% upfront, agreeing that the whole amount wouldn't work in this case. His friend thought that even 50% would be impossible, but after his initial nervousness, it worked and solved all his cash flow problems. This is less likely to work in B2B (business to business) and virtually unheard of in B2G (business to government). Terms are often 30 or 60 days. Stephen considers 45 days a workable figure.

Cashflow Finance aka Factoring

Stephen started his second business with $40k of his own money but then turned to factoring. Factoring is also known as cash flow finance or asset-based lending, and is available for B2B financing. Any receivable is treated as an asset, the same as your home or savings would be, and therefore banks and factors will look at the possibility of lending secured against them.

A factoring company advances between 75 and 90% of an invoice when it is raised, instead of you having to wait to get paid. The percentage depends both on your deal and on the debtor's credit rating. Stephen says that, in the States, they charge 15-25% – but maintains that healthy profit margins should cover that easily. This figure may seem pricey, but you should only make use of this sort of deal in the short term. Stephen grew the business from zero to $5m in revenues and, therefore accrued the profits he needed to fund himself out of the factoring deal within two years.

Stephen's experiences of factoring were very similar to my own. I used factoring three times, also for growth cash needs. On the second occasion, when my plans were the most robust, it proved particularly effective, and I was able to self-fund again within about eighteen months, with the growth accomplished.

It was still pricey, but much cheaper in the UK than the US. There is more choice now, so it can be advantageous to shop around for the best terms. The only danger is that at an agreed time limit of the advance, if the customer hasn't paid, the factoring company just helps themselves to the money back from your account.

However, despite borrowing being asset-secured, many factoring companies require a second, personal guarantee from a director. Some companies are less transparent than others; the third time I struck a factoring agreement, it was arranged by a VC contact who was hoping to buy the business. I was assured that there was no personal guarantee. I was stupidly trusting, and as that appeared to be the case, I failed to take legal advice before signing because "my friend" advised me. Yet sure enough, the next thing I knew, I had a complex and unpleasant personal guarantee around my neck. Always, always take professional advice on what you are signing.

Cash advances for emergencies

The next avenue to consider is cash advances. The charge for these can be as high as 200%, so clearly, they are only there for emergencies and very short periods. In dire straits, at one point in a business of mine, I took a loan from the only place I could get it – the back of a Sunday newspaper. That was not a wise decision, and I would advise never being tempted to go down that route. I paid ridiculous sums of interest for ten years.

Curiously, even success can leave you up against the wall when it comes to finance. Stephen Halasnik had one of the fastest-growing companies in the US, one that had generated a turnover of $7million in five years. He had a $650,000 line of credit with the bank. As he reached $500,000 into the line of credit, Stephen could see that he would need more to keep pace with growth. His mentor told him not to worry because of his track record and the equity in the business.

However, just at that point, his sales team had a phenomenal month, and Stephen could see that in two weeks, their payroll would be $19,000 short. So, he called his bank and explained how their growth was outstripping their funding and how he needed that $19,000 in two weeks. The bank manager was very upbeat, telling him, "Well done," that it sounded great, and that he would come back to him with an answer in 30 days.

Stephen was stuck. 30 days wasn't going to meet the payroll deadline. Factoring or finance from other banks would have taken even longer to set up. So, much as he hated to do it, he asked his wife's parents for help. Like many people who haven't ever had a business, instead of hearing 'cash flow was stretched because the company is doing well', they heard 'cash is needed so the business must be in trouble'. They said no.

Stephen talked to his payroll company about the problem, and to his surprise, they loaned him the money. A friend of his also offered a loan, and, of course, in 30 days, the bank came through. Even with a short-term loan, Stephen says that because he had taken a friend's cash, they worked harder and smarter. When you take money from friends and family, he contends, is the moment you find out what real pressure is like. They also did a deep dive into their collection process and achieved a 47-day average. Of course, another option would have been to cut back on growth, but like many entrepreneurs, Stephen didn't want to even consider that route.

Stephen believes that if the business is sound, there are always options.

Are banks even an option?

Once you have a track record, you can certainly try and borrow from a bank. They are interested in protecting their money and are almost entirely risk-averse. However, they will help if the opportunity is good enough.

One company that grew with bank support in the UK is Click Europe, a toy, leisure, and video game company. Ian Finch was only sixteen when he started wholesaling. He would get his parents to help him buy and sell products in The Loot, a magazine for selling things second-hand.

Ian started by continually phoning different companies around the world to see what clearance stock they had. He says he was a continual pain in their side. But it worked. He would get clearance offers from the big manufacturers directly, at unbeatable prices. For example, he would buy from South Africa Nintendo and get all the stocks they couldn't manage to sell there because the market was small but which could easily then be sold in Europe for huge profits. Royal Mail would tell him off for overfilling their letterboxes with packages.

His cousin, Steve Finch, joined him in the business, and they formed the company in 2005. At first, they were using their profits to increase the business year on year, selling on eBay and Amazon, and having smaller video-game-playing clients. But Click Europe started growing so fast that even their bank was impressed, giving them the overdrafts and import loans they needed to grow exponentially. From 2019 to 2020 alone, they managed to grow their

STARTFORSUCCESS

turnover by 65% to £26m, so the banks did indeed spot a huge opportunity.

There is no doubt that bank funding is rare. Asking friends and family for money brings a weight of responsibility that's uncomfortable at best, and at worst, terrifying. Cash advances are extortionate. Taking deposits direct from customers or using asset finance is a better alternative until you .

106

CHAPTER FIFTEEN

Crowdfunding

C rowdfunding can be a great way to raise money from friends and family. A huge additional benefit is that it also builds your brand, makes valuable contacts within your industry, and brings advice and support, as well as the cash. When it comes to crowdfunding, there are two main types: reward and equity.

Reward Crowdfunding

Lucy Gordon is the founder of From Our Cellar, originally funded with investment from her partner. However, when they decided to expand from the online service into supplying events, they knew they would need some extra funds and, equally importantly, to raise brand awareness.

Lucy's sister had worked for a crowdfunding platform, which enabled them to carry out the campaign extremely fast, and with expert guidance. They were only looking for a relatively small amount, to extend their marketing campaign. They successfully raised 125% of their target, and while they were aiming only at people they knew, they managed to bring in some previously unknown additional investors too.

Lucy says one of the initial advantages is that even if you feel comfortable asking your parents or best friends to invest in you, a crowd-funder campaign means that you can reach everyone. Lucy also found it much easier to say to people, "do go and have a look at our crowd-funder page", than send them to the website or ask them for money straight out. All the admin is done in one go, rather than processing each tiny cheque, which saves huge amounts of time too.

Lucy chose a reward crowdfunder, which is where, when someone invests, they can choose a reward. Lucy had been put off equity crowdfunding (giving away equity for investment) having watched her father's administrative difficulties with an extensive equity campaign. She had seen him become continually answerable to large numbers of tiny investors. Lucy wanted to save the equity for the people who would go on to work in the business further down the road. Nor do rewards force you to carry the heavy responsibility that equity investors bring.

The time factor is dramatically different from an equity-based, complex, and long-winded campaign, and it took Lucy only six weeks. Interestingly, not all the investors claimed the rewards. A family friend who was one of the larger investors wanted nothing in return, saying that they were simply excited to be involved. Others were offered various things from the website at a discounted price, yet some still paid the full price.

Lucy admits she was lucky to have her sister mentoring her. Still, she quickly learned that crowdfunding platforms do nothing to promote you, and if you want to raise the money, you have to make it happen by being continually active in promoting it. Another tip is to put money in at the start to get you up and running. It can be you that puts it in, your mum or your boyfriend, but only then will others follow. Equally, Lucy found there was a rush at the end when people realized they were nearly out of time.

Lucy recommends reward crowdfunding as a vehicle for family

and friends who invest, and especially for raising awareness. But it is vital to work hard throughout the process, making sure you are offering people the right incentives and reasons for investing in you and your business. Ultimately, this is what persuades people to put their hands in their pockets.

Equity Crowdfunding

Vicky Whiter came from a successful international corporate career, but after one re-structure too many, she returned home to her roots, near Stamford in the UK. By chance, she saw her local dry cleaners was up for sale and wondered if it would be a good business for her to run. Peters' Cleaners had been in the same family for generations, and Vicky felt that there was a gap in the market for out-of-hours cleaning. The more she looked at the firm, the more she also realized that their customers went there because they always had, and that the only time they lost a customer was when one died.

After only a few months, Vicky was convinced the business needed a radical change. It wasn't commercially viable, being people heavy and with the cost of labour having skyrocketed. Having been a commuter herself, Vicky also felt that stations were ideal sites for dry cleaners, if only they could be open early and late. So, she came up with the idea of an unmanned pod that would be available 24/7.

At this point, Vicky realized she could either "go big or go home." She could see dry cleaners closing all over the country, which meant an enormous opportunity for a new, disruptive model. Vicky pitched her idea to a group of business angels. They turned her down, telling her the idea for pods was too heavy on capital and that she had no clear marketing strategy. Vicky openly admits they were right about the marketing strategy and that it was part of the plan to find someone capable on that side.

Vicky and her husband committed some of their savings to take the next steps. Meanwhile, Vicky also researched franchising, which was another suggestion made by angels. She listened to audiobooks and soaked up knowledge as she walked the dogs, and asked her bank to put her in touch with a consultant.

Vicky had a lead investor, some funds from friends and family, traction in the market, and a disruptive business model. When someone suggested crowdfunding, it seemed a perfect match. She used specialists, IFQ, to help develop her crowdfunding strategy, and she says that the programme was crucial to progress the campaign on SEEDRS (an online platform for start-up investment).

By this time, Vicky was happy speaking with passion one to one, but crowdfunding is a mass-marketing exercise. Vicky went on LinkedIn, networked with contacts, and put an ad out for a marketing expert to join their board. Within a few days, she had an application from Clare, who Vicky thought was way out of her league but who assured her that building a brand from the ground up was precisely what appealed to her. One of Clare's many genius touches was their slogan, "Drop your trousers". It was a great icebreaker when Vicky was pitching and made them stand out. A great slogan will always increase your chances of success.

They raised a healthy amount through the crowdfund, but Vicky went back to angels for the balance. With the marketing plan in place and having followed all the advice, Vicky raised the balance of what she needed – and one additional advantage of having done the crowdfunding first was that company's value was set, so the angels could not argue with it.

Crowdfunding for exposure and early adopters

Elnaz Sarraf, the founder of the hugely successful ROYBI Robot, grew up in Iran and was one of the first people in the country to have a computer. She even began to program at five years old. She saw her father running his own company and her mother working behind the scenes on the finances and operations (because women were not allowed to work in business there at that time).

Elnaz raised $4.2m in a seed round for her business idea: an educational robot. Elnaz and her co-founder wanted a place where any child can learn based on what interests them and helps prepare them for a brighter future. They needed something tangible to show investors. So, the two of them had to knock on factory doors till they could convince one to make a non-working prototype.

From there, they could move on to the most challenging part of their product development, structuring their artificial intelligence algorithm. ROYBI Robot has several AI components, such as voice recognition, face detection, and emotion recognition, working in combination to enhance the child's learning experience.

The company needed to start with a colossal impact to make the business viable. They used a crowdfunding campaign through Indiegogo to sell products to early adopters and raise awareness through word of mouth and press coverage. Within one month of launching, their crowdfunding campaign received recognition from Time Magazine as one of the best inventions in education that year, followed by two further cover features.

Even then, things didn't go smoothly. They manufactured the hardware six months ahead of schedule, working day and night and sometimes even sleeping at the factory. But when they started shipping the first batch, they realized that they had a significant Wi-Fi problem in some of the products. They had to stop the shipments, unpack thousands of units, do updates and repack the products. It was challenging, but they successfully fixed the problem and regained their customers' trust. ROYBI Robot is now available in major retail stores, and has customers in over 30 countries.

Which one to choose

From these three stories, you can see that the benefits of crowd-funding are significant, and money is only half the story. It is also now a mainstream way of raising funds.

For smaller amounts, reward funding is easier and quicker. Equity is complex, can take anywhere up to two years and will cost you a chunk of your business. Both approaches need marketing expertise and guidance through the crowdfunding process. However, both bring huge brand exposure and, often, investors with industry knowledge.

CHAPTER SIXTEEN

Equity Investors & Pitching

O utside friends and family, the success rates for pitching for finance are low. Whatever route you choose, you have to market both yourself and the incredible investment opportunity you have on offer exceptionally well.

However, angels and even VCs look at deals much earlier in the business cycle than they used to, so choices appear numerous. Your first step is to divide those who invest into start-up and pre-trade, then early growth, post-revenue, and finally full-on growth. Pitching a PR start-up to a VC that only invests in post-revenue is only going to waste your time and theirs. Gain clarity, too, on the type of investment you are looking for and then the specific investor profile that will work best for your business.

Equity investment takes a long time, whatever route you choose. Never fall into the trap of leaving it till you need the money. Most courses of action take a year or so to plan and prepare.

Preparation

Investment is a business with both regulated and unregulated people and companies. Therefore, it is wise to ensure you work with those conforming to the regulations of the financial governing body of your country, for example, the Financial Conduct Authority in the UK.

The next thing that can go wrong is that all too often, the small start-up does an initial balance sheet themselves or goes to a friend of a friend who knows some book-keeping to do it. Balance sheets need to be set up correctly for investment, showing not just what money has gone in, but if it was in return for equity or a loan. Getting this wrong could kill your chances before you have even begun.

Investment is a specialized area. Going to a specialist accountant and solicitor early will pay off because all the articles, sale rights, and agreements with any shareholders will play a positive role in your pitch. Investors need to know precisely what percentage of the company is actually going to be owned by them and if it has been set up for investment tax relief.

Getting the valuation of your company wrong is an almost guaranteed route to failure, and too often, early-stage founders do not understand the structure of a balance sheet and a company's capital set-up. It is a colossal mistake. Investors are more interested in what money has gone in and the value of similar companies than they are in over-enthusiastic projections. They are pretty disinterested in business plans altogether.

The valuation will also determine how many shares you are going to have to let go of, so it must be genuinely defensible. While too high a first valuation may sound fantastic, it can cause problems for Series A funding down the line. However, most over-optimistic valuations kill investment potential.

Raising investment is the same as inspiring any other group of people. You are presenting to individuals who will react to different things, prioritize different facts, or simply go with their gut. You have to respond to all of those demands.

An excellent investor-ready deck matters, and that means not one that jumps up and down shouting "hey, look at me, I'm great", but rather, one that is focused on financial fundamentals and then investment opportunity. A strong value proposition in your market is crucial. Investors want to make money. They know the risks are high, so they need to be convinced by the opportunity. The greater the market opportunity, the better chance of higher returns, and a 3-10x return is the only possible way to make it worthwhile for investors to take a risk.

Investors will look for how strong the marketing proposition is, and how you are planning to access the market and sell your offering. This is challenging. However, when it comes to raising money, potential investors will be looking for a detailed insight into the market's potential. SAM, TAM and SOM (see marketing) analysis can help you here.

Calculations of market shares at start-up or pre-revenue will be shaky. A start-up may not have a year's trading, or the growth rate could be so extreme that it will throw the equation off. With established figures, forecasts will become both more accurate and more useful. For now, there is some degree of guesswork, and investors know this. But showing the relationship between those three and the growth potential still demonstrates solid reasons to start, grow and invest in a business and, equally importantly, that you understand them.

Investors also look for the strength of the team. People invest in people. They prefer it when there are at least two people on the management team, and they look for proven management experience. They are not impressed by anyone who intends to give the business only their part-time attention. Equally, investors are savvy, and as we discussed earlier, non-experienced founders who claim to be capable of being CEO (and/or other titles too) fill them with deep suspicion. They would prefer someone experienced and independent on the board to ensure that their investment is in safer hands – and that means you have less autonomy.

Pitching

Founders are often nervous about pitching, not least because they want to keep all the details of their idea to themselves, convinced that they will be stolen. But investors are not looking for ideas. Instead, they are looking for opportunities – and if you don't give them enough inspiration and information, they will simply not invest.

Part of that faith is gained by you knowing what you are talking about. Anyone can memorise a presentation on making a spaceship, but only experts in that field could take an open Q&A session on it. Q&A sessions are your chance to shine, convince your audience, and show that you are the real deal.

Creative pitches are more likely to stand out and be remembered. Investors sit through a staggering number of pitches, and not surprisingly, become quickly bored when they see the same old thing being presented in the same old way. A little sprinkling of the "drop your trousers" type will ensure that yours is not just another run-of-the-mill presentation, if it is done well enough and in small doses.

One start-up's data will sound similar to another's. Presentation is vital, but it has to be a different, innovative presentation that communicates your idea. Add a little theatre, a little magic, something to entertain and make you stand out from the crowd. Your personal story may be part of it, your brand may be another, but you need to show something that demonstrates you are a person they want to do business with.

Beware of any lack of transparency. Discovering during due diligence that someone else owns all the IP or that there are substantial unmentioned director's loans, or litigation that hasn't been disclosed, destroys the trust that's essential for the deal to go through.

Pitch Competitions are fierce.

Nicolas Naigeon found this out when he entered The European FoodNexus Startup Challenge, which offers growth opportunities for Food and Agtech start-ups in seven European countries. The challenge was "How to feed 10 billion people in 2050", and Nicolas was pitching the Aveine wine aerator invention.

Nicolas and his co-founder realized how much they had misjudged the competition as soon as they arrived. The hall was packed with inventors offering showy presentations of their rainwater purifiers, harvesters, and other innovative ideas that achieved the goals of reducing food waste and optimizing agricultural yields. When Aveine joined up with the other French competitor, both had to laugh as they discovered they were both presenting an invention around alcohol. Despite their good humour, though, they were also very intimidated. Trying not to panic, the French inventors brainstormed a new approach to make themselves sympathetic to their audience while also becoming better showmen.

The presentation was going well until they were asked how their invention was going to change the world. After a long pause, Nicolas had a flash of insight and announced, "with us, we drink less, but we drink better." This became part of the brand for Aveine, and they focused on drinking in moderation, but also in luxury.

The lesson here is research, research, research. If you are pitching in a competition or to investors, the more you know about what is expected, the better your chances.

The Zen factor for your nerves

Even very experienced CEOs can get nervous. Dominic Drenen, now the Managing Director of Sumo Energy, was preparing to deliver a presentation to potential investors a few years ago that had the potential to result in a colossal acquisition deal. He was concerned about whether he could instil the right levels of confidence and inspire with his vision. Determined to increase his chances of success, Dominic took the unorthodox step of hiring Tony Nicholls, a highly experienced journalist turned media trainer. Good Talent Media is a full-service media agency that has trained hundreds of business leaders for successful presentations.

Tony uses a mix of philosophy and techniques gained through decades of meditation and time spent in 'silent retreats' in India. This philosophy of taking yourself out of the narrative, of removing the 'I,' means that speakers can tap more deeply into their true selves and connect with their audiences as a result. Speakers fall down when they start thinking about themselves. The focus needs to be 100% on the audience.

Tony suggested to Dominic that he concentrate on what the potential deal would mean to people and how it could help Australian families. It made all the difference. The presentation was a resounding success, and Click Energy was sold to Amaysim for $120million.

Tony finds that, courtesy of COVID, everyone has an underlying level of anxiety, and that they see this more and more with CEOs at the lectern. But if you are looking for the X factor in a pitch, the zen factor is a proven solution.

Pitching and presenting

Don't be overconfident and underprepared. Begin early, get advice from experts, research endlessly, prep well, pitch brilliantly – and have a plan B, as realistically the odds are more against than with you. Recognize that you are far from alone if the thought of pitching makes you nervous. View it as you would any other new business task and get expert help.

Finally, because the chances of success are small, it is easy to get overawed and become willing to take any deal. That could bring disaster, but this doesn't mean that the lowest-cost option is necessarily the best one either. The overall deal matters. Your early investors set the tone for your company's future...

CHAPTER SEVENTEEN

Angels

Angel investors are people who want to invest their own money in early-stage businesses. Many were entrepreneurs themselves and are now looking to give back, and profit in the process. Angels do not have unlimited funds, so there will be times when their wallet is firmly shut, no matter how exciting your deal. Equally, many prefer to invest in sectors they know, which may rule you out automatically – so it pays to do your research and find out that information before approaching people.

As with all fundraising, the more you research, the more you understand how the investment world works, the greater your chances of a deal – and more importantly, the greater your chances of a deal that is right for you. One way of gaining that in-depth knowledge is by becoming an angel yourself.

Looking from both sides of the table

Laura Harnett is the founder of the household essentials brand, Seep. Laura chose the route of become an angel investor to learn how to start up and raise investment for a company. She had held a number of senior retail and advisor roles in the corporate world, but on recovering from cancer, Laura decided she wanted to stop playing things safe and do things that made her happy. She had mentored in some accelerators and was continually amazed by the speed of the start-up world, where decisions are made fast, as opposed to taking eighteen months and endless meetings.

Laura did an introductory angel investment course with UKBAA for £150 and then joined an angel syndicate called Angel Academe. She learned the importance and mechanics of the UK tax advantages for small businesses under SEIS/ EIS schemes for her potential investors. Many professional investors won't consider investment in the UK without that being in place, so that alone opened up the field of possibilities when she came to seek funding for Seep.

When Laura started Seep, she needed to raise seed funding to cover the high stock levels she needed to compensate for long supplier times. She had not got the time to go down the crowdfunding or VC route and she was reluctant to bring new investor board members into her business, which often makes raising institutional investment essential.

Laura also initially found it challenging to ask friends, family and contacts for investment because it felt like a big ask. However, she learned early on that if she spoke inspiringly about the company, her vision and how she was making a difference in the world, that was the best way of raising funding. People advised her to not think of it as asking for money but instead re-frame it as offering people an opportunity. Laura quickly expanded her network with people who asked to be told when she was fundraising. About half the raise came from this sort of contact.

Sitting on both sides of the table taught Laura a lot. She has learned to ask for help, that it is better to send an email than prevaricate, to try something rather than aim for perfection, not to overthink things, and to constantly talk to everyone about the business. These result in plenty of people waiting keenly for the next fundraiser. Also, she says, slow and steady wins the race every time, and you have to learn to prioritize ruthlessly.

As an angel, she started out by investing in founders that she liked and paying less attention to the numbers. Quickly, she learned that was a mistake, that she should look for sustainable traction, and that unsexy businesses can be excellent investments. Finally, she found out that some companies are not made to be investable. Not every business is set up for a massive sale or to offer great returns for investors, but they can still be good businesses.

Pitching on a pavement in a deckchair

Charlie Cook is the founder of Rightcharge, a company that helps EV drivers find the right charge point and energy tariffs. Charlie had worked in both the physics sector as an engineer and gained energy and electric vehicle consumer market experience working at an energy supplier. He spotted a gap in the market. Despite the EV industry being set to rocket, there was no online comparison site for EV charging.

In 2019, he started Rightcharge while still working at his old job two days a week. By the time he raised first-round funding, the pandemic had fully hit, and everything had to be done remotely.

About 50% of the money came from friends and family, but Charlie also had other investors. One was a Tesla owner who happened to live on the same road as Charlie, and who had just sold his own global software development company. They had chatted in the pub, but the official pitch took place over a beer, on two deck chairs on the pavement outside Charlie's house. In addition, a few other contacts from the industry who Charlie pitched to via video link came in, meaning that Charlie was able to reach his £100k target.

When it came to raising a second round in 2021, many original investors put in more, which often happens if angels are happy with how their investment is performing. Charlie planned to crowdfund the balance but abandoned the idea when Terry Lee, CEO of Tesco, expressed interest and offered to put in a big chunk of what was needed. But the deal fell through due to a conflict of interest and Charlie was faced with needing to raise another 300k in a month.

Like Laura, Charlie wasn't interested in giving away the total control demanded by interested VCs and was delighted to find another investor who was already in the comparison market. But Charlie's lawyers took a week longer than promised to draft the deal, by which time the energy crisis had hit, and again the deal fell through.

Charlie had been at 900k at one point; now he was down to 500k again, which was just enough, but "not a great feeling". At this point, he received an invitation to connect with a VC in Norway on LinkedIn. They exchanged messages, and the VC asked Charlie to let him know if he was ever fundraising, to which Charlie replied that they were closing the current raise that day. The VC didn't waste any time, and agreed to an investment of 100k. The deal was signed in 48 hours, and the money arrived within five days.

The vast majority of the funds invested in Charlie's company came from either the automotive or comparison site sectors, a perfect example of looking for investors interested in your sector.

Quasi-Angels

Disruption is terrific, but sometimes it can be challenging to find the right investors. Jade Francine, co-founder of WeMaintain, was confident in their new approach within the elevator market, but knew they needed more industry contacts to develop their business network. She and her co-founders had just returned from Asia and the US, and had few contacts in real estate in Paris.

So, for their seed funding, they approached people in the industry who would have the contacts to leverage. Problems set in because these people were not seasoned business angels. Jade says that they naively thought it wouldn't matter, and that the value of their network would outweigh their limited knowledge of the start-up world.

The first problem was that they misunderstood how start-ups' valuations work and demanded a portion of the company's equity larger than that which experienced business angels would have asked for. Secondly, they wanted control over all basic decisions.

Jade refused the offer. The business angels who joined them eventually might not have had the previous industry experience of those that they rejected, but right from the beginning they offered vast business knowledge, great insights and a shared vision. Jade says it taught them that saying no is as important as saying yes when it comes to fundraising.

Your Investor, Your Choice

Angels will often be your first investors. The relationships you have with angels, and the culture of those angels, therefore, are crucial. They will set the tone for your business. Getting this wrong will never be worth the cash. Be ready to walk away from deals, rather than sighing with relief and taking the first sum of cash that you're offered.

Always fully check out your possible investors. Consider looking only at accredited investors, or at a minimum, ask for references and chat to other founders they have invested in. Check that they have the knowledge, the connections, and ample cash so they don't get twitchy at any point. Find out in full what their skill set is, and their strengths. At this stage, you are looking for a package deal, not just the cash.

Find out how involved they want to be and get to know them to see if you can be honest with them and trust them. Ensure your goals are aligned. At some point in the future, they will want to realize the profit, and if you have alignment from the start about an exit plan, it will save many horrors later on...

Social media can be a powerful tool for networking, getting your story out there, and fundraising; this has become even more true since the pandemic. Charlie is one of many who have found success on LinkedIn. In the early stages, angels are still looking for people to invest in with inspiring stories, and LinkedIn provides a platform to tell those stories. Twitter has also had its share of success stories. Networking, as we have seen, is crucial at the angel stage.

You can do most of the finding of investors yourself if you are careful, and courses to help cost little, but when you use a professional advisor, use a specialist one. Always learn the tax advantages in your country. Also, use angel websites, directories, networks and associations, and networking events. Within your own industry, networking can be less of a lottery, providing they know how investing works.

Finally, understand that most people opt for angels for the great relationships and knowledgeable advice that they can bring and stay away from ones that want too much equity and too much control. Not all of them do.

CHAPTER EIGHTEEN

Venture Capitalists

Venture Capitalists (VCs), operate in consortiums, venture capital firms, and as individuals. Some also operate as angels, investing smaller amounts and re-investing further down the road if the company performs well.

VCs are looking for big returns. They focus on whether the proposition is strong enough and the marketing differential is significant enough. But with tech valuations still huge figures, it appears that more and more companies around the world are offering that potential.

VCs have a poor reputation

All investors will want their money back at some point. They will usually know when that is and look for deals that they think will make it a reality. One problem is that timings can change, and they might want their money back earlier than expected. Seasoned VCs will put this stipulation in the small print, which you may well never see.

I have both heard and experienced for myself some horror stories at the hands of VCs. The problem is that non-disclosures are signed early, so many of these stories do not go on record, nor reach the light of a court. And in any case, VCs are more at ease in a courtroom than most of us and have the resources to fight you if they choose.

Not all of them are as bad as the ones I had the misfortune to find. Some are nearer the side of the Gods. But always be realistic; they are there to make money, not to make friends.

Is the reputation of VCs justified?

Tim Mercer, the founder of cloud technology business Vapour, knew next to nothing about raising finance when he first started. Tim says one of his rookie errors was not asking for enough during his first raise so that when he had to go back for more rounds, he had already set the level of equity. He could have got more and given away less.

Tim thinks that the bad name that VCs have isn't always earned. They are, however, often people who have never run a business themselves, but because they happen to be whizzes at balance sheets, they are determined to tell you how to run your company. Tim has had one outstanding experience of a VC firm. All VCs enforce accountability, and this one insisted he report monthly on precisely what was going on under the bonnet of the business. That process means he always knows exactly what is going on in the business, which has proven invaluable.

On the downsides of VCs, Tim cautions that no VC has ever offered him a terms sheet that matched what was eventually agreed. It may be something minor, a small percentage change, or a slightly different management fee, but there is always something. When you query it, their answer is always that it must be a mistake so he should just sign it now, and they will add an addendum later. Tim always refuses and gets it re-done. He says to remember that they want the deal as much as you. With your first deal, it is easy to agree, especially when you are excited about the offer and want to get the deal done, but never rush. Tim's investors have all been with him long term by following these policies.

Tim's biggest issue came when they wanted him to have a Financial Director. Tim says that in retrospect, he should have hired someone part time, but instead, he did what was asked and gave away equity to get someone full time. Two years in, the gap between what he wanted (a long-term business) and what his co-founder and the FD wanted (a fast exit) was widening and, worse, destroying the company culture. Tim went to his investors and gave them an ultimatum, saying "either these two go or I will". His investors reluctantly agreed, but told him that they would sell the company if he was wrong. But Tim trusted his gut, parted company with both, and surpassed his investors' expectations.

The investment world is a small one.

It is important to continually be aware of the people you meet on the circuit. Roman Grigoriev pitched for seed capital for his company, Splento, a high-quality video and photography firm, at an event put on by the VC firm Galaev & Grierson. Two of the investors he pitched to were Dragons Tej Lalvani and Nick Jenkins. Tej invested but Nick passed on the investment for various reasons, including his commitment to Boomf, the personalized greetings company founded by (as she was known then) Kate Middleton's brother James.

Several other VCs had invested in competitors, so they stayed well away from them at the start, focusing on investors in their own sector at later stages. They kept in touch with Nick, and when it came to their next finance round, they asked him if he would like to be their lead investor.

The outcome was completely different. Instead, a consortium of investors, led by the founder of the VC firm, Septan Galaev, and Roman himself, bought out Boomf from Nick, James, and their shareholders. Boomf had been hugely successful but had been hit by COVID, and this re-booting was the perfect step to turn it into the leading player in the greeting cards and card-attached gifting business.

Roman paraphrases the Steve Jobs quote saying that you can only connect dots looking forwards, not backwards but you have to trust the dots will connect in the future. Sometimes in business, the least expected, but wonderful thing happens, something you could never predict and can only see when you connect the dots backwards. But these wonderful things come from building connections.

What to look for

Shem Richards of Goldilocks Suit has worked with investors at every stage of development and found that investors within funds tend to be hands-off to start with. The ones who have stayed with him through the rounds have become more influential and active, though eventually, that drops off again.

Like Tim, Shem finds many VCs started a business twenty years ago, if at all. Everything is now changing so fast. If you had a product a few years ago, you had to gear everything to the big retailers. Now you can succeed in selling direct to customers, especially since COVID, but many VCs haven't grasped that yet.

Equally, once, if you did not have a patent, you didn't have a business. Now it is more of a grey area, and there are other ways to protect a business, especially with technology such as AI, software and machine learning sectors, which are all particularly difficult to patent. Shem has found it is sometimes necessary to explain these other options to an investor. You could spend a hundred grand on a patent that will take four years, by which time the tech will have changed in any case, or a different strategy altogether will have fundamentally changed the sector.

Overall, Shem says not to be surprised if you know more than the VC about your specific business niche, and to never compromise your strategy or business idea to suit what was ideal twenty years ago. You should know your business best. Good VCs are not that interested in the what, but are all about the why.

Shem looks for conviction in a VC. Other investors who are just looking for a 10x return in three years will probably not bother to support you. Great investors don't put money into a concept, product or founder because they believe them to be a sure bet; they just have to believe in them enough.

A mixed bag

As always, these different experiences reveal mixed reports but many common themes. Of course, all investors want the best deal they can get. It is a question of how far they will go to get it. They will all want to carry out due diligence. However, some will bombard you with demands for so much information and for so long, that you are both exhausted and, at the end, so desperate for the cash that you will take any deal on offer.

Do your research. Be aware from the start what a small world it is. Build your contacts. Be exceptionally wary about every deal, and about every tiny detail in the deal. Be prepared to deal with out-of-date advice, to fight for what you believe in and to ensure that you have the leeway to do so. Be ready for onerous reporting demands, but look at them as a learning opportunity. Never forget, you are there to make them money.

Testing, Testing

Business ideas come to people in different ways, at different places, and for different reasons. Some come because they are looking for something themselves and can't find it, or it does exist but only at an inferior level of quality. That may mean they are onto something.

However, equally, it may not – and it is the blind conviction that your idea is a winner that leads so many businesses astray. They get so wrapped up in their own excitement over the brilliance of their idea that they go full steam ahead without doing the one simple thing that could save them from disaster: talking to enough people to be sure that those people want their potential product enough to pay for it.

Finding out if people like a product idea can be hard, just like raising money without a prototype. So, in this section, we look at what pretotypes and prototypes are, and the costs and returns involved.

We are also going to look at how crucial it is to position yourself correctly in the market and absolutely nail your differential, rather than be lost in a sea of similar offerings. Instead, the aim is to be the star, offering something above and beyond. Finally, we discuss that trendy buzzword: disruption. We look at what it means to be disruptive, and how to successfully run a disruptive business.

CHAPTER NINETEEN

Evaluate the Potential

If you are launching a new business, or a new product or service, it is essential to research the market beforehand and avoid letting excitement carry you down the wrong path. Rushing from the idea into prototyping or starting up and trying to sell can be costly disasters. Far better to spend your time talking to customers and working out ways to assess and capture demand; because unless you have something people want, badly, and a big enough market, you have no viable business. Your conviction of brilliance has no basis.

You need to knock on as many doors as possible, have conversations and get as much feedback as you possibly can, before laying out too much, or ideally any money. And soak up every fact and figure available on your market.

Valuing your market potential on paper

One way to evaluate market potential is using TAM, SAM, and SOM methodologies of calculating potential market share and revenue. Useful to show investors, these are also helpful methods for working out if it is worth entering any new market and for planning your marketing and sales strategies generally. The system divides and refines the potential market through each process. Don't let the acronyms put you off.

The starting point is TAM, which stands for Total Addressable Market, in other words, the total market demand for your product or your service. TAM provides an understanding of the growth potential and is the absolute maximum business that you could generate in that market. It is calculated by taking the total number of customers in the market and multiplying it by their average spend. Working out TAM is all about market research and using existing data. Throughout all three processes, the better your research, the higher the accuracy.

SAM stands for the serviceable addressable market within that. For one reason or another, you won't be suited to the whole TAM market. Price, geography and style differences are just some of the reasons. Calculating SAM is focused on the part of the market you are a good match for. Concentrate your research on the total number of potential customers that would be a good fit and multiply that by the annual average spend of those customers.

Finally, the smallest area is the SOM or serviceable obtainable market. It is unlikely you will have all the customers to yourself, even in a neglected part of the market. There will still be competition. For SOM, divide your last year's sales by the SAM to see what your market share was that year. Take that market percentage and multiply it by this year's SAM.

That may sound complex, but once you have gotten your head around it, you will have a really sound grasp of market potential both for starting up and for any planned expansions.

Low-cost product testing

If your product is low cost, it is not viable to spend too much on market research. Paris Michailidis is co-founder of My Little Panda, a business with a wide range of re-usable and sustainable household products. He has to ideate all the time and says he always looks at potential new ideas through the eyes of other people. He narrows down his ideas by talking to people and putting himself in their shoes. He finds out which benefits they like or need, and works from there, never telling them the full idea. Only when he has refined the new product completely does he develop it.

Paris gave me an example. Over the years, he had heard so many people complaining about having to match up socks after washing (or about losing one of a pair), so he developed a product that sticks socks together during washing.

Paris's research may be less sophisticated than that of some huge companies, but the principle is the same. It will just take your time and shoe leather. Remember the Steve Jobs quote "Just think about the customer". It is always about the customers' needs and perceptions.

Testing products at pitch events

Abe Matamoros, co-founder of the innovative pillbox Ellie Grid also agrees that talking to everyone is vital and they did exactly that with its market research. Abe sees some entrepreneurs fall into the trap of going out to try and convince people they need to use their product, which is the opposite of what they should be doing, which is listening and letting them tell you what they need.

Abe says that many people are embarrassed to show something that is not the finished product, while others are worried that their ideas may be stolen. He found kick-starters to be really useful for testing ideas, not least because they are time-focused. Abe has seen people fall into the trap of taking so long developing the perfect product that the market moves on long before the product can be produced. The real test is always if people will pay for what you are producing.

Another trap people fall into is confusing enthusiastic friends and family with customers. Many of them will believe that they are doing the right thing by encouraging you, telling you what you are doing is wonderful, and even buying something. The truth might well be that they think it is a terrible idea. Friends and family should never be your source of feedback. You need honest, unbiased opinions from a broad cross section of potential customers.

The better your use of data, the more progress you will make. At the same time, you should be researching the demographics of your customers to get a clear picture of who you are targeting and what their problems are. Data, be it on product development, customers or financials, is so crucial, yet in the firefighting that running an early-stage business involves, it is often the thing that gets pushed to one side.

The rare exception

Just sometimes, a successful product gets started more by luck than design. A few years ago, Jessica Flinn of Jessica Flinn Jewellery had picked up two steel wedding rings from a local manufacturer for a customer who was getting married the following week. To her horror, she lost them whilst juggling with her six month-year old. Total panic, they were nowhere to be found. Not wanting to let their customer down, her husband went out to his shed and taught himself how to make steel wedding rings. It took him two solid days to recreate what Jessica had bought.

These days, their Flinn and Steel alternative metal wedding rings account for nearly a third of their turnover, and while they are no longer made in the shed, her husband still designs them. The original rings turned up a few months later.

On that occasion, it worked – and most importantly, the customer was happy. But if you developed a product off the back of one person liking it, you could be in for some costly disasters. Get feedback first.

Customer feedback over experts every time

Sharon Melamed started Matchboard because of her natural love for bringing people together and a logical extension of that was to create a B2B matchmaking business.

To test her concept, Sharon spent the first month mocking up her idea with screenshots and showing it to potential customers, choosing people who fitted the profile she planned to target. Matchboard has two sets of customers, both buyers and suppliers of business services, so Sharon consulted both. Buyers immediately loved the idea of a site where they could enter their needs and, at no cost, get a supplier shortlist that met those criteria. Suppliers wanted to be matched with potential buyers. However, what they wanted was to pay if and when a deal was done as opposed to for any lead or on a subscription charge.

Experienced business people cautioned Sharon against this "success fee" approach, saying that suppliers would never be honest about advising when deals were closed. However, Sharon's gut feeling told her that if you give customers what they want, the business will flourish. So, she built a radical business model based on trust. The feedback was so overwhelmingly positive that she went straight to full launch without any sort of beta product.

Nine years later, Matchboard has 4000 clients, including many of the world's most recognized brands. Sharon says that it was refreshing to learn that people are more honest than you think, and most still do the right thing, especially with an incentive. In their case, suppliers knew that if they built a strong relationship of trust with Matchboard, they would benefit from more leads. Sharon ignored the experts, followed her instincts and found success through listening to what the customer wanted.

One step forward

The first step is to look if there is enough market potential by cracking your data and figures. No market, no business. The second is to do your market research. Only then can you position yourself right in the market and be sure of offering something that customers want to buy.

So many people tell me they are struggling with sales. However good you are at selling, you can't sell something people don't want. More often than not, it isn't a selling problem, but an idea problem – something no one wants.

CHAPTER TWENTY

Prototype, Pretotype & IP

Once you have had this wonderful brainwave about a product that will revolutionize everybody's lives, it is easy to get stuck choosing the next steps to take. How do you get that customer feedback without something to show people? Google can be your friend, and the processes and costs involved in product development can be staggering, but that feedback you must have. The more you test, the less money, time, and effort you will waste. Before going any further and spending any money, get feedback on your competition and find out what works, what doesn't, what your customers like and what they don't like

The biggest mistake you can make is spending money without feedback. But how do you develop a product without spending a fortune and risking someone stealing your brilliant idea? One answer might be to pretotype.

Pretotyping

A pretotype was so named by an ex-Engineering Director of Google called Alberto Savoia. He became involved with Stanford Technology Ventures Programme and started working with Richard Cox Braden and Tina Seelig, who lectured at the Hasso Plattner Institute of Design. Savoia used the theory during his time with

Google, and the three of them refined it into a set of tools and techniques to help inventors and innovators test out products before they built them.

Pretotyping is designed to stop people from falling into the trap of building something the market doesn't want, a test to see if people will use it when product development is complete. It is about taking as cheap as possible a mock-up of your idea out to the public and testing it out on them. Pretotyping is massively cheaper than prototyping. You can also get inventive and apply some home-grown solutions.

Innovative ideas for product development

Paris Michailidis, the co-founder of My Little Panda, sells a vast range of innovative and relatively low-cost household products. He says that while many entrepreneurs go to a prototyping company, who do the designs and then find a manufacturer that requires investment, Paris wanted to bootstrap. So, he had to take a more economical route to develop a product to take it to market without paying to achieve it.

Paris took a crash course on graphic design. He met some brilliant graphic designers there, with whom he became friends. As a result, he is constantly learning and also has superb advisors.

The next stage was replacing the expensive trial product. Paris' suppliers are 20,000 miles away, so going to a factory to discuss what he wanted was not a viable option. He took time to get to know the people over the phone and on video calls, and says it has been all about relationship building. He dismissed the easier option of using third parties because it wouldn't have had that personal element. Paris doesn't pay for samples, and third-party testers get paid on sales profit. Instead, he trades news and information about the UK markets in return for the manufacturers' time, so the suppliers are alerted to possible market changes. Paris never promises success of products either, telling his manufacturers straight that trying out new products is like a roundabout. You just have to try one exit and see what happens.

Paris's first product took nine months to develop. It was the only time he has ever paid for any design element. Even then, his approach was innovative and economical. He created a competition for students and offered £500 to the winner, a low price for what became thirty different designs, and the students benefited from having proven designs on their CVs. The most challenging part is always finding a manufacturer to produce a sample. Paris says a combination of a sales pitch and lots of kindness usually wins through.

Hopefully, Paris's innovations will spark some ideas of your own. For many products and services there is no need to invest huge amounts to build trial products and you can find other ways around it.

Prototyping

If you are as sure as you can be that you have tested your product idea in every way possible and got all the feedback you possibly can, some products might call for the prototype route. The more expensive and complex a product, the more essential prototyping becomes.

A prototype is focused on testing the product, working out if it should be built, how much will it cost to build, and whether it will do the job it is intended to do. While, at the end, you will have the genuine article to show customers, the money invested can be colossal.

Full-on prototypes go through many stages, starting with a conceptual sketch, a digital drawing, and a virtual prototype in 3D. Depending on your innovations and skillsets, you might take it this far on your own or use a professional prototype designer. Expect to do this repeatedly, finding faults, refining, improving, and adjusting to feedback. This stage also includes researching trading standards and market restrictions.

Manufacturers of products involving complex tooling or engineering do not do free samples. It isn't worth their while. If you are paying a manufacturer, you want to develop a partnership that works for mutual benefit. For tech companies, you may do an early build yourself and employ more sophisticated skillsets over time.

The complexities of product prototypes

Matt Leach's experiences are a good example. Matt had served as a Royal Marine Commando, then decided to train as a doctor. When he was a student at UEA, he went over to a friend's place on his motorbike. Matt had a bike lock with him but could find nothing to lock it to. He was only there five minutes, but when he came out, the bike had gone. During that year, he saw friends fall victim to the theft of bikes, snowboards and laptops, among other things. Matt could see there were two problems: easy-to-cut-through locks and sometimes a lack of something to lock to. So, he started playing around with designs. Once he had a concept, Matt sold the VW camper van that he had bought on leaving the Marines to cover the costs of the initial prototype for his lock.

Not only did the prototype look like Frankenstein's monster, but it cost tens of thousands of pounds. Matt's partner James had marketing experience which meant he could do the necessary 3D animation of the designs they needed to pitch for outside investment. Matt says that "At the start, you have a vision in your head, but you are the only person who can see it – especially till the prototype gets better – and it is incredibly hard trying to get the idea across to angels".

They spent three years and £250,000 taking their smart lock, The Limpet, from concept to a full-blown prototype. Matt says that unlike apps where, if you want to change something, you can do it from the comfort of your own living room, with prototypes, you have to change the design; then, the 3D model is printed again, and then everything is re-tested before spending thousands on tooling. Matt also found the development process a battle because a lot of people they dealt with thought Geotekk statistically wouldn't be around in a year, so they took the money whilst they could. The start-up failure rate is huge, so you have to learn not to hate the player; they're just trying to get paid. You've got to learn to play the game.

IP and Patents

IP and patents are highly complex subjects. Take specialist advice from the start, and keep copies of every sketch, date stamped, along with getting anyone you show the entire idea and product to sign an NDA (non-disclosure agreement).

Patents are applied for when you have a physical prototype, and they will cover your processes, outlines, mechanisms and properties. For patents, it is crucial that you don't release anything into the public domain before you file as it will be classed as prior art and therefore unprotectable. Investors will usually insist on your prototype being covered by patents, but patents may not be the right option, especially in tech.

If you decide to spend money on protecting your idea and design, use an expert and expect to pay ongoing monitoring fees to monitor global imitations, and to take the action that might be needed. It depends on your level of investment if patenting is worth it and how quickly it will all change in any case. Patents become worth it depending on the level of investment and providing the market will not be changing too fast that what you are patenting has already had to change.

Elon Musk believes that patents are lottery tickets that only give lawyers more to fight over. He says that if someone comes along and makes better electric cars than he does, it will be a better thing for humanity. It depends if you can afford to think like that.

CHAPTER TWENTY ONE

MVPs

However brilliant, however excited you are about what you have in the way of a service or product to start with, it is unlikely to be what will become your fully developed version; the version that you will be entirely happy with.

Enter the practical option of an MVP or minimal viable product. This is your early-version product, and it is minimal because it has the bare minimum of features needed to make something sell. MVPs combine income and testing. If you try and self-fund through every development stage, you can run up a massive debt. A lot will depend on your existing skill set. If you know what you are doing, for example in tech, it is possible to develop an MVP on a moderately low budget. Indeed, this approach is more common in tech, but the principles can be applied to other companies.

MVPs and the big brands

The MVP is a crucial part of the process of market validation. You can engage with your customer market to get genuine feedback on what the customers like (and don't like) about what you are doing. You get to understand what has value, which immediately puts you ahead of the competition and refines the product as you go along, but all the time you have some money coming in.

Mailchimp earned its way to success in its early years, offering existing customers a free version of their new software and a premium subscription service for a superior version. This meant they could fund growth and retain total ownership of their company.

Apple continually used MVPs. Early capital came from a box enabling people to make free long-distance calls. Apple1 wasn't their perfect product, but it was a step on the way that paid for them to stay in business. It is hard to believe that the original iPhone was an MVP by some people's definition. It was, at that moment, incredibly different from the products of their competitors, with its touch screen, and the way it could support a full web browser. But while it only had a few apps and no ability to load more, no notifications, and many other features didn't appear till later, nor did their competitors so it did not present a problem. What was crucial for Apple was to find out if people could manage without a keyboard and if the internet would really work on a mobile phone. So, they focused on those critical elements, only adding others later. Remember that Jobs himself used to say "you've got to start with the customer experience and work back to the technology".

This is the key to a successful MVP, and should be the foundation upon which you build a more extensive business. For example, a real-estate agent might sell houses and become successful later on building them as well. The kernel of their business would still be selling houses.

The benefits of stealth building

Rich Wilson is the co-founder of Gigged.AI, a digital sourcing platform that finds top tech talent and puts together project teams taking advantage of the boom in the gig economy. Rich had a background in technical recruitment and a passion for connecting people. He and co-founder Craig Short were convinced that AI could make contingent hiring easier. Gigged.AI was, as Craig describes, a brand built by stealth.

Rich and Craig stayed in full-time jobs while building their MVP so they could build both business and product with no cash flow pressure. Instead, they each put in £5,000 of their own money and managed to secure a £100k innovation grant. This funding gave them the means to test out the beta AI product. A beta product is a pre-release version given out to a group of users to test, but with actual user conditions. Now, having gone through the alpha in-house tests, they could evolve further using customer feedback.

Gigged.AI has kept its initial marketing outlay low and used LinkedIn to connect with people in the industry. They spent £800 on a billboard in London that read "The 9-5 is dead", alongside their logo, photographed it and posted it on LinkedIn, and sent it to journalists. This was a disruptive, low-budget approach that paid off because they had been offered seed funding and had 3000 users on their platform within three months. Up to this point, both founders and brand had stayed in the shadows, but they then met for a coffee, agreed it was time to quit their jobs, and step into the limelight. Their emergence created a massive buzz and meant they walked into a thriving business by stealth building their product and brand.

Beware perfection

It is all too easy to get obsessed with perfection in business – perfect products, perfect photography, ideal customers, and giving them what they want at any cost. What you should focus on is making money in a sustainable way and growing your business, not perfection. MVPs are a way of making money while you focus on developing your product, your vision, plan, and value proposition, and they provide you with the opportunity to get to know your market at the same time. An MVP has to have enough value for the customer to pay for.

Serial software entrepreneur Matt Bullock discussed MVPs with me. He described how he had often fallen into the trap of trying to perfect something special to meet every customer's individual needs when he first started. Now he is wiser, and while he might make a couple of minor alterations for a great customer, he won't invest so much time if it isn't financially viable.

We all chase customers and deals. Matt told me of a deal he was negotiating with Vodafone through IBM in his early days in business, which involved giving them the rights to the IP. The negotiations were taking most of his time and holding back the rest of the company, so Matt decided to walk away. If the essence of your product is right, and it appeals to the majority of your potential users, it isn't necessarily wise or even viable to mess around with it.

I had a similar experience with a massive brand with shops in most large towns throughout the UK, who wanted me to manufacture bespoke products to sell under their brand. On paper, it looked like the deal that everyone dreams of. Their design team was full of suggestions for modifying our existing products, but of course, they wanted upgrading and to pay less for. The mark-up we would have made would have been so minimal that the risk wasn't worth taking on. Like Matt, I walked away from a huge deal with no regrets. You can get carried away with big talk of vast market share, but at the end of the day, you need to be making money.

Changing MVP s for one customer, however large, is not worth it, nor what an MVP is about. It should be about developing your sweet spot: the magic bond between the consumer and the core element of the product. Does it give pleasure – and does the basic version work? With those two things nailed, the extras can and will be developed naturally over time.

CHAPTER TWENTY TWO

Differentiation

In overcrowded markets, it is every entrepreneur's worst nightmare that no-one finds their business, or that no-one remembers it after they have found it. Ensuring you stand out from the crowd is the secret sauce of marketing and one of the crucial ingredients of this sauce is the concept of differentiations.

Your values, vision, branding, design and how you deliver what you do are all part of potential differentials: the things that make you, you. All of them should show up in the way you design every product, the way you deliver your service, and the way you do business. USPs are what differentiate you from the competition in terms of features or benefits that they can't get from the competition. Your value proposition is a clear statement of how the customer benefits by choosing you.

Price can be an area of overlap. Poundland wouldn't be Poundland if it wasn't for their prices and this is also their USP. But it really only works if the pricing difference is extreme, such as with Poundland. Just being good value wouldn't have the same oomph at all.

Differentials offer the customer more, either directly or by association, and make customers feel they have to come to you instead of anyone else. They are developed from a cross between your strengths and your customers' needs.

Apple is always an obvious example of successful differentials.

Apple has always stood out from the competition, with a brand and design differential so strong that it knocked all the competition into near obscurity. Highly disruptive companies that do things completely differently to the traditional market are by definition successful at differentials. The dating app Thursday, where people only meet up once a week, is a case in point.

USPs are usually easy to replicate, so they need continual monitoring and updating to be effective. Make your brand differential strong enough that imitators pale by comparison.

Outstanding differentials make strong companies

Developing USPs and differentials starts with knowing absolutely everything you can about your competition in the marketplace. What is their price structure, what do they do well, what do they do poorly, why do customers buy from them, what makes customers unhappy with them? These are all questions you should know the answers to, and in detail. Obsess about them, find out why they win deals and why they lose deals.

The challenge with a product is that it is nearly impossible not to produce something similar to another product already on the market. Indeed, if you haven't got any competition, you should be asking yourself if there is any demand. If your whole brand is different and your products and services reflect that, then that makes them stand out.

Your differential has to have a Wow factor. Semi-good won't cut it. So, for example, if you are going for a price differential, many people think it is ok to say, "we are cheaper than most of the competition". That will leave customers stone cold. Only the extremes that are mega-different – the Woolworths, the

Poundland, The Dime Store – succeed making these extremes part of a differential that counts.

If you already have investment behind you, you probably have developed a core differential because it is one of the main criteria that investors look for. Outstanding data analysis is the key to success, telling you what works and what doesn't, enabling you to keep expanding and developing differentials.

A different way of doing things

Differentials should be deeply embedded into how you do everything you do. Olly Richards was an English teacher and jazz pianist when he chanced upon the power of stories to help learn languages. With no business experience behind him, he hesitated for several years before turning his idea into something commercial.

One summer, years later, Olly had just come back from a holiday in Egypt, and decided to try and take the concept further. He sat at his parents' kitchen table and wrote a book of short stories in Spanish for people wanting to learn the language. He then self-published it with a $10 cover, knowing nothing about writing, let alone publishing. But it did exceptionally well, so Olly expanded it to other languages, translating the book into German, French and Italian.

Then one day, by chance, he saw a Facebook message in his junk mail from someone he had never heard of. They wanted to talk to him about his "readers" so he assumed they meant his blog. It turned out the message was from the publishing director of Teach Yourself, an imprint of Hachette Publishing. They told Olly they had intended to produce their own graded "readers" (graded books that help people learn a language), but having seen Olly's ones, they had decided it made more sense to collaborate. The books exploded into bookshops everywhere, eventually growing into a collection with more than twenty titles.

Anyone involved in writing knows that it isn't a hugely profitable career, and Olly still wanted to develop a business based on language learning through stories. The books showed traction in the market, and people were continually asking him where they could find a course. The problem was a chicken and egg one: for someone to read a story, they need a level of competence to start with. So, Olly was stuck, but not defeated. He was sure that the very different way of teaching a language with stories would outshine the traditional methods.

It took him two years of experimenting before StoryLearning® was born. People loved it. He has since developed that original course into ten more languages, and it remains the core of the business. Having established an exceptional way of being different from the crowd, they can sell related products. They have developed what Olly describes as an entire business ecosystem, in the same way as Jamie Oliver has for pots, pans, and knives.

What was originally a simple concept, with work, testing, customer feedback, and more work to be done, emerged as StoryLearning®. It had such a strong differential from other languages courses that it not only stood out, but found massive success.

A customer service differentiation

Sometimes your point of differentiation can lie in your customer service, especially if you are in an industry that has not traditionally been associated with anything but sales. Emma Parkinson has set her company, International Energy Products, apart with this differential, disrupting the sector that supplies specialist alloys for the oil and gas industries.

Emma had no experience of the industry other than being a recruiter who specialized in engineering. One of her clients persuaded her to jump ship and, with no metallurgy or engineering knowledge, start an entirely new career. It is a sector where most women are only found in admin or sales, and while Emma raced up the career ladder, it was made clear that there was no space on the board for women. So, Emma then started her own company, specializing in raw material supply and sub-contracting cutting services in order to be able to provide a comprehensive service.

Coming from outside the industry, Emma had a different interpretation of service than was common in this sector, which was purely reactive, just to receive and process a customer order. Emma saw things very differently.

Emma says that her level of pro-active response was vastly different from day one. She sees what they do as a support system for their customers; one that responds to their needs immediately. The accountant may have to wait 'til tomorrow, but never a customer. If she is out on site, she still responds via her mobile. The industry is, she says, a dinosaur, making it easy to stand out. Most suppliers are big corporations with mountains of red tape and huge distances between them and the customer.

Emma's company is more agile and more versatile. Their secret is that they put themselves in their customers' shoes and ask what they are trying to achieve, thus aiming to be a solutions provider. For example, a customer buying large volumes as and when needed may receive inconsistent quality in their orders. International Energy will agree to a deal where they hold what is needed for the year, resulting in a win on both quality and service.

Emma wants their customers to get more business. To achieve this goal, if someone rings up with an order for a certain size, it's policy for International Energy Products to ask what it will be used for. Every new team member shadows Emma when they join so that they deal with inquiries in a way that matches Emma's own standards in this.

By finding out about the job, the company can often offer a better deal or a faster alternative. Perhaps the customer is ordering in bulk, but their own machines can only cut at certain sizes, so that they lose massive amounts in waste. By providing a cut-to-size option, the company makes it possible for their customers to save money.

Alternatives

There are many differentials to be found, and the greater the differential, the more you will stand out. They are always a combination of relevance, good design, the memorable and the authentic – and above all, they are completely different to everyone else, not just in your eyes – but in the eyes of your customers. Which brings us to disrupting...

CHAPTER TWENTY THREE

Being Disruptive

We are in a disruptive age – disruptive in the types of business, the way we do business, and the ways we behave in business. Disruption is perhaps the ultimate differential, and is by nature innovative, though innovation is not always disruptive. Disruption appears in product, service and brand. Disrupters aim to change the market status quo, doing something that achieves the same end but with a fundamental change in approach. The speed of development in the tech sector has allowed disruption to happen faster, and more disruptors are coming up behind every existing business.

Disruption doesn't just happen by chance, and disrupters do not only achieve what they do by knowing their market before disrupting it. A great example is Uber, which changed the face of the taxi business. They succeeded by identifying customers' pain points – having to walk rainy streets searching for over-priced taxis – and so they delivered instead a taxi service with an entirely new model.

To be a disrupter takes confidence and belief. Many of us are resistant to change and say things "can't" be done. Your whole team will need to think disruptively and thrive on disruption. When hiring a new team, it is easier to find creative, innovative people who buy into disruption. It is harder to change an existing team that is set in old ways, but more and more new disruptors are finding colossal success.

Disruptive Dating

The first time I saw George Rawlings was on an Instagram post, standing in a London street, wearing a homemade sandwich board announcing that his girlfriend had dumped him for cheating on her. George and co-founder Matt McNeill-Love had just started a dating app called Honeypot. This particular marketing stunt cost them £300 and earned an initial 5000 downloads. The style became a trademark of their success.

They had set out to use buzz marketing because it was affordable. It took a couple of goes before they nailed it, using stories that provoke emotional reactions. People became involved with the stories, which is the key to disruptive marketing. Sadly, lockdowns at the start of COVID were not conducive to the dating sector. But ever determined, George and Matt decided to respond by turning an old idea about dating on its head – and new ideas are what disruption is all about.

Thursday offers something unheard of in dating: only one date night a week. Its reach has been phenomenal. Drew Barrymore was filmed talking about it in Hollywood, which is a pretty crazy level of success from low-budget marketing.

When it came to pitching for finance, Thursday's founders created a homemade video shot in an elevator and sent it to hundreds of angels via social media. This was radical too, and it worked. Angels bought in, including the founder of Monzo, Tom Blomfield, who had disrupted traditional banking a few years previously. In a world of traditional banks, with high street outlets, power-crazed managers, piles of paperwork and huge costs, suddenly along came Monzo. Like Uber, success came from knowing the customer's pain points.

George's LinkedIn is a constant stream of disruptive marketing moments – including the new Thursday marketing assistant with her own sandwich board. Thursday breaks all the rules and is immensely authentic; that's why the market loves it. New brands in other sectors are copying their unique style. Their differential is woven into everything they do.

Disruption with a book

Daniel Flynn, Justine Flynn, and Jarryd Burns started Thankyou with a mission to end world poverty. The Australian success story has been achieved at least partly due to a disruptive approach and the ability to think outside the box to solve problems.

Phase two of Thankyou's growth programme was an expansion into New Zealand. They had a target of AUD 1.2m and decided to use a reward-based crowdfunding campaign. Daniel wrote a book about Thankyou's journey to that point, calling it "Chapter One". It would help, but even bestsellers in Australia see sales of only 5,000 copies, so it wasn't going to go a long way to hit their target.

The solution was a disruptive one: to release the book in a way that hadn't been done in publishing before. They set up a pay-what-you-want model. They wanted to reframe the question in people's minds from "how much should I pay for this book" to "how much am I willing to invest in an idea that could change the course of history?"

When the pitching day came at the retailer, their cover wasn't even ready, Daniel could feel resistance and that the pay-what-you-want-model was proving a challenge. The retailer was questioning how to manage the barcodes, which are linked to price, till one of them peeked outside the box and said that to change the game, they would have to start thinking differently.

To Thankyou's delight, less than 24 hours later, they not only had a book deal for the model they wanted but also full front-of-store display, front counter displays and advertising space. The book exceeded their expectations and raised an incredible AUD 1.4m.

Customer pressure

Daniel has become well-known for his disruptive marketing and unconventional campaigns. His approach is to harness the power of like-minded people and their actions to bring about significant and long-lasting change.

In Australia, 75% of people shop in either Coles or Woolworths. Five years in, Thankyou were launching new products and had meetings booked with the supermarkets to pitch the new ranges. To ensure their success, Thankyou launched their Coles' and Woolworths' campaigns, by asking their supporters to take short videos of themselves saying that if the retailer stocked the Thankyou range, they would both buy it and upload it onto their social media.

This answered the vital question that any retailer wants to know before they stock your product. Rarely do they get guarantees, so of course, it worked.

More customer pressures

Not only is Wilfred Emmanuel Jones incredibly focused, he has always been a disruptor, too. Commissioned Market Research companies threw up their hands in horror at the idea of his brand name, "The Black Farmer," declaring that people would be offended, but Wilfred welcomed the attention.

Wilfred was also battling to get in the door of the supermarkets, and the ace up his sleeve was a clear understanding that there is one thing supermarkets fear: the customer. So, he built a website with a page called "Petition" and put links on it to all the leading supermarkets. Wilfred then launched a massive marketing campaign, both digitally and with a countrywide, tasting roadshow. Everywhere he went, he asked people – if they liked the taste of his products – to sign up and ask their supermarket of choice to stock it. The supermarkets gave way to customer demand.

Commonalities

What all these examples have in common is that the overall aim (be it getting into a supermarket, funding a business, paying for a lift or arranging a date) is still much the same as it has always been: By looking at things from the customer's point of view – looking for their pain points and their needs, and questioning anything and everything that is done "because it always has been like that" – huge successes can be achieved.

Even the most traditional industries can be disrupted. Get it right, and it can unlock doors to success beyond your expectations. Whatever the product, service or marketing strategy, disruptive ideas and differentials are the magic that attracts investors, employees and customers alike. Focus on those, and you open yourself up to all sorts of possibilities.

Reaching Your Market

Even a brilliant and disruptive setup won't achieve success if people don't know you exist. You cannot ever just sit around waiting for your customers. Instead, from day one, you have to go out and find ways to ensure people hear about you. Or to be precise, the right people hear about you, people who are likely to buy from you. The magic combination of identifying who those people are and creating something they want, always circles back to you having listened to them in the first instance.

Marketing isn't just about hiring someone with social media savvy. To grow a business, you need to hone and develop your marketing abilities. Clever marketing is the art of getting people talking about you, and crafting that conversation to be so interesting and engaging that the people they talk to join in and want to talk some more. Great marketing creates a movement.

That takes communication, emotional connection and using language that resonates.

Depending on your business, you may still have to sell to your customers, but in a collaborative way rather than the hard sell of old.

Once you have your core customers, you treat them so well that they go out and shout about you too. Happy customers form a band and then a movement, and they all join you, shouting about how amazing you are. It is as simple and as hard as that.

CHAPTER TWENTY FOUR

Understanding Marketing

Marketing is part science, part art. It is about identifying the customer and market's pain points and needs so that what you do responds to them; totally understanding your customers; creating a brand personality and differentials that your market cannot resist connecting with; building emotional rapport with your customers; talking to them in their language, and keeping them interested; it is also about measuring each one of those things, costing them, and at every moment, knowing which bit of what you do is most effective for the company.

It starts with listening to the customer, and aligning with them by positioning yourself correctly in the market.

How positioning can make or break your start-up

Richard Mabey is co-founder and CEO of the legal tech company Juro. He says he learned the hard way that starting a business is about understanding your customers and communicating with them in the right way.

When they started Juro, Richard and his co-founder understood the product they were building but had forgotten to research whether anyone actually cared about it as much as they did. They also failed to convey the value of what they were offering.

Their first website was put together with what Richard describes as spit and chewing gum. They couldn't afford fancy designers or developers, so they built it themselves. The first iteration was a mess. To paraphrase, it said something like:

"We've got this great software which uses some clever automation that has something to do with legal contracts; you might be able to use it. Now, pay us money."

They waited for leads, but they weren't forthcoming. Richard says that their positioning was woefully wrong. They hadn't fully understood the problem it solves for people, nor who those people were. Traffic was surprisingly good, but they had no conversion.

They had to go back to basics with their customer discovery. They conducted interviews with customers, in which, rather than talking at them about the product, they asked questions about their customers' lives. They asked what jobs they needed to do, how they currently managed tasks, why their current software couldn't help them, and how that impacted their day.

Richard says they became obsessed with their customers. They asked more questions about which jobs had done be done daily, and which were their priorities. They asked what time their customers started work and what software their colleagues used. Then, Richard and his co-founder used all that insight to change the website and gear it towards their customer needs.

Soon, Juro was seeing more leads than Crufts. Their target prospects landed on the website and could answer 'yes' to questions like: "Is this a product for me? Does it solve a problem I am experiencing? Is it valuable to my team and me? Does this start-up I've never heard of get me?"

These are great tester questions you can try on your website. Richard says that while this probably looks basic in hindsight, many founders assume their idea is so fantastic that they ignore getting positioning right. He re-iterates how important it is to understand that your assumptions as a founder matter much less than what a customer actually needs. If you want your positioning to work, just ask customers what they want. It's hard to overstate the phenomenal impact that empathy and forensic market research will have on your success.

Juro recently completed a multi-million Series B raise, increasing their valuation fivefold. In 2019, FT Intelligent Business named Richard as one of the top ten legal technologists in the world.

The different aspects of Marketing

Mark Hayward is founder of Sway PR, specialists in media relations, who get massive exposure in major news channels for their clients. Mark believes that you cannot ever use one form of marketing in isolation and this was one of the reasons why he studied a range of marketing functions and became a Fellow of the Institute of Marketing. He believes in using PR in tandem with PPC, branding companies, social media specialists, and SEO people. All of these elements have to fit together, and Mark uses this principle with their own marketing hence the recent re-brand from Sway Communications to Sway PR.

Mark says that with marketing, everything starts from three questions:
- what are you selling,
- who are you selling it to,
- and what is your point of difference.

Communications can only work and work effectively if those answers are aligned. Before reading on, check if you have the answers to all three questions clear in your mind for your business.

Success results from a combination of visibility (people being able to find you) and your credibility (what people say about you behind closed doors). With PR, you have to be clear about what you are trying to achieve and what message you need to get across. The difference between PR and advertising is that advertising communicates the idea that you are good, but with PR, a journalist is telling the story about you and that brings much more credibility. Measuring results is always the next step in the process and Sway PR measure how many people see their articles in the news combined with a rating system for all the publications. But that is still only half the story.

While it is great to see your company in a premium publication, you need to measure the ROI (return on investment). This might be visitors to your website, or inquiries or sales. Every step requires measuring success.

Measuring and growth

Sustainable growth comes from having the right volume of demand for what you do and then you delivering it better than anyone else. The bigger that demand, the easier growth will be. We have talked about the importance of nailing your differential and value proposition as part of your strategy, combined with getting to know every bit of your market or markets. When it comes to measuring for marketing that knowledge has to be segmented, for different markets, different products and different customer profiles, so you optimize ways of reaching and connecting with each one. You also need to know the cost of acquiring all your different segmented customers. Effective marketing is a lot about measuring, otherwise you just flail around doing a little bit of this and a little bit of that, hoping something will stick.

Why bother with different segments?

It is easy to focus on just one market and do it well. But the risk is higher because the market may change, or some clever competitor might come in and leave you scrabbling.

Identifying different niches and segments also means that you may find some areas where you have an even better fit, and easily beat the competition. Looking out for new opportunities, new niches and new markets should always be part of your marketing strategy. Niches are often under-served because the big suppliers don't find them worth the effort, and this creates opportunities for you.

Identifying a niche comes from identifying additional customer needs. For example, a travel business might be selling holidays to Europe but then drill down and find a neglected niche for yachting holidays. A store selling particular types of fishing hooks would be a niche within the overall fishing market. There can be several smaller niches within a single market, and each have enough potential. But the last thing you want is to build a whole new website devoted to European yachting holidays or specialized fishing hooks only to find that there is a demand, but only minimal demand.

You can develop niche markets with organic growth by positioning yourself as an authority in your subject. If you are recognized as a leading expert on fishing hooks, that is an immediate attraction to anyone buying. So, talk about your subject everywhere: online, in forums, on podcasts, and in person at shows and exhibitions.

Nailing the buyer persona is a big part of the strategy for niche markets. You need to know that buyer intimately. There has been a recent move away from segmenting by age and gender demographics to analysing customers by their needs and desires, and I think this trend will only continue.

Talk to the customers and find out where they feel things don't work, or what they want but cannot get. Look for needs that aren't being met. Crunch the numbers and find out if you have discovered some fool's gold or a rich seam to mine.

CHAPTER TWENTY FIVE

Getting People Talking

For people to talk about you, there has to be something interesting for them to talk about. It is that simple. And creating something interesting to say means creating stories, encouraging debate, creating a buzz.

Initially, your job as a leader will be to share stories about why you started, or why you developed some particular product, to share your vision and your values.

Sometimes the storytelling is written, and sometimes it is spoken, which can be another challenge for entrepreneurs. But the challenge comes in two parts – the right story, then the right delivery.

Story first, product second.

Jarie Bolander has over 20 years of experience bringing innovative products to market. He is also an expert PR and Marketeer, podcaster and author, and through the combination of those things has come to believe that well-told stories can change the world.

Jarie says that one constant in his twenty-five-year-plus career in start-ups is that the path seems to have been random, chaotic even. But with the gift of hindsight, he can see that it was not. The constant in his entrepreneurial career has been that the companies that told the best stories found success. The actual product appeared secondary to the story they were telling.

Jarie says this revelation came to him when he worked with a company called Sutro, which he was helping to scale. Sutro is a water testing robot for pool and spa water. The product was good, but the challenge was how and what story to tell about it so that customers connected. Jarie explains "Humans love a good story. Each of us has survived on planet earth because our ancestors told the best stories. Through stories, we understand the world and can avoid the saber-tooth tigers. This principle holds for products as well."

From water robots to storytelling

Jarie was also looking at stories from a different viewpoint. The holy grail of start-ups is product-market fit, and this is where he sees most start-ups go wrong, working on the principle of knowing it when they see it. Jarie, and Sutro founder Ravi Kurani, wanted to scale the business economically.

They wanted a story to ensure they achieved that, so they used their engineering backgrounds to formulate a process that measured the effect of their stories and showed what worked. What they did for Sutro led them to found what became their latest venture, The Story Funnel.

The Story Funnel aims to align your products to your customers' needs by delivering your message in story form. They help ensure that the story is clear, concise and inspiring, with clear values that people want to align with. The Story Funnel is a SaaS tool that uses Machine Learning to help get the right appeal to draw people in, starting with an emotional hook.

Jarie and Ravi scaled Sutro's revenue from nothing to seven

figures in twelve months, and then doubled it six months after that. There is so much noise out there, and the one way you can overcome that noise and stand out is by telling the best, most unmissable story. Growing a business is so much easier if you get the story right and develop your ability to tell it.

It's not just what you say; it's the way that you say it.

Mark Hayward never planned to be an entrepreneur. Instead, he was very happily running ski-chalets in France when a friend from university contacted him and said that a leading PR company in Manchester needed some help with the sort of work they had been doing while at university: He came home.

One night in the pub after work, his friend said, "you know, we could do this our way, and do it better". They wanted to focus on the best possible added value for the client, and so 1090 Communications was born. Built in only three years, it won numerous awards and they then sold it for a satisfactory sum. By the time Mark and his friend had worked out the agreed handover time, Mark was married; he spent his sales proceeds traveling with his wife. Starting in Tokyo, they returned two and a half years later from New York, enjoying experiences from the peace of the Galapagos to getting caught in riots in Peru. On their return, Mark took a job back in PR, but after a horrendous health scare, decided to move house, have his first child and put family first by working for himself again.

Mark says that some people consider PR to be a part of Marketing and some vice versa. Mark always views the whole picture, but sticks to what he does best - PR. Mark shared some examples of what they do to show PR at its best.

Stirring up a debate

When Primal Adventures approached Mark a couple of years ago, they wanted to create an entirely new niche type of luxury ultramarathon, run over 120 miles of the Scottish Highlands. It was a new concept, alien to traditional hard-core runners. Mark and his team took three major media players to the Highlands – the *Financial Times*, *City AM*, and the *Sunday Times* – to give them a taste of the event to come. They were coached by expert advisors, even the current world champion, and they completed a part of the ultramarathon route every day. The trip generated three significant pieces of coverage, including a cover story in the *FT* and a double-page spread in the *Sunday Times*.

But Mark had identified a debate between old-school hard-core marathon runners and the new luxury-focussed athletes. He encouraged this discussion, which was picked up on radio stations, then the BBC. It spread internationally into Europe, Asia, and the USA. The founder of the marathon was always on hand to chat and reinforce the message that marathons and luxury are not mutually exclusive.

The return was phenomenal; tickets cost around £15k per person, yet they had one hundred athlete enquiries generated through the PR.

A global story

A second example Mark gave me spun from him meeting Jonny Cooper, who, back then, had a company called The Adventure Tour Company. With Mark's help, they would re-brand and become Off the Map Travel. Jonny had just returned from a self-organized trip to see the Northern Lights in the Arctic and wanted to help others to do the same. At that point, Artic travel was still very niche.

Mark created a range of quality national media coverage, including a Telegraph announcement of the best possible times to experience the Northern Lights in the UK, with expert viewing tips from Jonny. The articles were so popular that, at the time, they were the most shared travel articles on the Telegraph website. The Met Office picked up on the popularity and started to also monitor space weather for possible Northern Lights activity.

Mark then recruited a network of PR people in Australia, Hong Kong, Singapore and the US to form a Hub-and-Spoke model that took the campaign global. The Sway PR network saw his team research and write press releases, gather images and package everything together in the UK, before sending them to his local consultants around the world. Their job was then to use their specialist knowledge to recreate them for their local markets and drive media coverage there, optimizing contacts and getting stories in front of the right people. The system has made the reach of Mark's agency immense.

Successful PR comes from long-term strategy, creating opportunities for people to read about you over an extended period of time, but sometimes you just hit gold.

Fans and Power Users

You start by telling interesting stories and then other people talk about you. These other people may be the media, but you are also aiming to create a fan club of the sort that David Meerman Scott talks about in Scale for Success. With sufficient buzz, a fan movement takes on an impetus of its own, and the people within it carry and create their own narratives and stories.

Tech has its own version of this: the power user. These are people who have used the products for a while, know them well and are both the biggest fans and the first to point out any issues. To define who is and is not a power user you will need to find your own specified level of purchase or usage. These customers will have been with you from early on and have plenty of experience of what it is like to be a customer. They are also very vocal. However regularly they use you, if they hide silently in a corner, they are not power users. A combination of the amount they share and their degree of knowledge sets them up as an expert and influencer with power over how others then react to you. Their feedback is likely to be on the nail. Their spend is, of course, welcome, but it is how they spread the word that is their special value.

CHAPTER TWENTY SIX

Emotional Connections

S uccessful brands create emotional connections with their buyers – emotional connections that are so strong that they want to identify with a brand; be part of its journey and its tribe. That can be challenging to do for a start-up with little or no experience and even less budget. But building emotional connections can still be achieved – providing these connections are steeped in both values and vision.

It's all about emotions

Joe Seddon graduated from university with the grand sum of £200 left from his student loan and a conviction that access to higher education needed significant disruption. The result was Zero Gravity, a social mission that mentors' low-income students into top universities and careers, and a brand that has emerged into the public eye from the humble beginnings of Joe's original West Yorkshire bedroom.

From inception, Joe was convinced that the secret to success lay in branding. A Gen Z, Joe grew up admiring disruptors such as Uber and Deliveroo. On the flip side, he looked at education and saw that no one had changed anything, that brands had no connection to emotions at all.

By this time, Zero Gravity had a small board of private investors, and Joe had a hard time breaking the news to them that he wanted to spend 30% of their initial investment on branding. None of them came from a marketing background or could see any reason for a start-up to spend such a massive percentage of its available cash on what they saw as a logo and a few other brand assets.

Meanwhile, Joe had seen and been hugely impressed by the brand revamp in Leicester Square. Joe found the company responsible, a small branding agency in the East End specializing in travel. Joe could see no reason why they couldn't do an equally successful job for Zero Gravity.

Self-therapy

The agency and Joe started by looking at the consumer, asking questions such as "what do they feel about the world?" Joe drew on his own pre-university memories and explored what mattered to him, what made him emotional, what he believed in. They would then question how the brand represents that person.

The next stage was to broaden the research, and they invited ten students from Zero Gravity's platform in and asked the same sorts of questions: "What's your journey been to this point, how do you feel about it, and how do you feel about your future?" Joe says it is because brands are intangible that it is always so important to start with this very tangible research and evidence.

Even when it was all defined, things didn't always run smoothly. One of their main marketing videos was an endorsement from former Labour leader, Ed Miliband. It was an outside shoot in Miliband's North-London garden, and they had forgotten the British weather. The end result was Ed Miliband standing talking in torrential rain and a ruined shoot. All part of the learning process.

Joe saw the results of his conviction when Zero Gravity disrupted the European Brand Awards to win three awards alongside massive global giants like KFC, HSBC and Mastercard. Zero Gravity has since raised a seed round of £3.5m from investors. Brand, as Joe says, is nothing without people's emotions.

Emotional Ambassadors

Jazz Gill never dreamed of being an entrepreneur. He had an excellent job as a software engineer that he was reasonably happy in. But then he saw a "stick in a bucket" concept at a local gym and knew he had to take it to market. This product would become the SPARBAR®, a boxing and fitness device that simulates an opponent. It would also lead to his fitness brand.

Jazz says that you are very, very green and trusting when you start as an entrepreneur. It feels like an alien world, and while there are plenty of people on hand to help, some give you good advice, and some do not. Over time, your radar improves.

Jazz had more than his fair share of knocks after starting in 2013. He lost the company at one point, had to sell his car and wedding rings, and bring his new-born daughter home to a mattress on the floor. He tried every traditional route he could think of to get support for the product with no luck: growth Hubs, sports companies, distributors... no one was interested.

The break came when he marketed the SPARBAR using local kids. Many had problems, and one particularly needed his help. Despite being penniless and with a company to try and manage, Jazz started what is now their Ambassador Programme to help. When a video they had shot got shared, it went viral.

The Ambassador programme has become the focus of all their marketing and motivation, and it has seen Jazz through all the tough times. They have kids from inner cities and some from abroad. He and his team visit the gyms, hold brand meetings there, and mentor the kids. Those on the programme are then invited to attend shareholder meetings. Each is given a piece of equity in the company and is taught about investment. Jazz calls them his investors and sees his role purely as an enabler who is getting to experience a little of their journey. He lights up when he talks about the kids, and it is clear that this is his vocation. The relationships are hugely personal and authentic.

Money that would have been used on traditional marketing instead goes into the programme, developing community gyms and sponsoring schooling for African child athletes. Everything they do is based in their shared values of diversity, inclusion, change, and impact. This is crucial to create common ground between the partners, and the ambassadors' stories both represent the brand and perfectly reflect the brand values.

Consumers see the authenticity of the brand and its extended community. The more the brand succeeds, the more good they can do, and Jazz has the knowledge that they make a difference every single day.

Jazz met resistance to his idea at first, as some others couldn't see where the benefit of the investment was. However, Jazz says that the ambassador programme has turned out to be the secret sauce without which they would never have scaled to where they are today: the SPARBAR is now world famous. The company has come a long way from being down to £8.00 in total funds, and that success came from building a brand with emotional connection.

Two different stories

You will develop an array of stories surrounding your business. There will be the start-up story, the story you have about your future aims, and those that surround your people or your customers, your product or your community. It is about finding the right ones for you, the most powerful and emotive.

Creating emotional connections is done in two parts. The first lies in the research to understand what matters to your audience; what will tick their emotional boxes. The second is about communicating messages that will move those emotions. While neither easy nor quick, finding that emotional connection is a gamechanger.

CHAPTER TWENTY SEVEN

The Power of Language

S teve Jobs used to say, "The most powerful person in the world is the storyteller." You have to have the story but then you have to tell it. Storytelling is an art and an ongoing requirement as a business owner.

The first story you share is the one behind your brand, where you got the idea from, or why you started. Some PR companies will leap with enthusiasm about how they will work with you to construct the most brilliant of backstories on your behalf. I get hundreds of them by email every day – and trust me, most of them are dire: dull headlines, same old content, no authenticity, and no emotion.

Whatever the story, learn how to tell it. You have to create the ultimate page-turner – on the web.

A masterclass on the business idea story

To share a masterclass on how to tell the story of "how I got the idea for my business", I turned to Olly Richards, founder of StoryLearning®. Olly's story starts with the headline:

"I stopped breathing at 3 am in a village on top of a mountain."

Want to know more? Of course, you do! That is the sort of headline that sets you apart from the crowd. And every word after that is crafted for anticipation, bringing the picture of his near-death experience alive. He talks about that night in detail; how, in South America, he went out with friends, ate steak and drank Malbec, before waking up at 3 am struggling to breathe. There was the horrible panic that followed, desperately trying to get oxygen into his lungs, while watching the haunting view of the valley, and wondering if this was where everything was going to end for him.

On that mountain, we are with him as he is trying desperately to calm himself down. We see him grab the only book to hand, which happened to be in Spanish. And, of course, it makes perfect sense to us that he would remember some of those stories the following day.

The way the stories stuck in his head gave Olly the idea to explore the power of using stories for learning languages. He went on to learn eight languages himself, develop a methodology to help others learn languages through stories, sell hundreds of thousands of copies of his books, and build a hugely successful business that partners with some of the largest organizations in the world.

His achievements are outstanding. As entrepreneurs, we know just how much effort and hard work that takes, but that isn't what makes Olly and his brand memorable. From the moment I came across Olly, I remembered him as "the guy who had his idea on the top of a mountain." The story works because you saw the mountainside, felt his terror – shared his emotions.

Ongoing conversation

You can open a film with a sensational trailer, but if what follows is sufficiently dull, you can still end up with people walking out in droves. The next skill comes in keeping customers engaged, talking to them, offering them the additional value they don't get somewhere else.

Georgia Metcalfe founded the French Bedroom Company fifteen years ago. It has been named a UK Cool Brand for five consecutive years, and Georgia's clients include international celebrities and royalty.

Originally, a birthday trip to France found her coming back with a gorgeous French bed and an idea. She knew there was an appetite for French beds in the UK and thought she would set up a side gig. Georgia saw that women's lives were changing. The cost of living had risen, and they were no longer sitting at home drinking tea. Instead, they had become time-poor and had no appetite for slogging around stores looking for beds at the weekend. Having studied tech, she was able to build a non-transactional website to show off the product, and she called in favours for a location for the shoot and a friend for photography. It cost her £500 to launch.

Georgia knew precisely how she wanted the brand to be from the start: communicated through fantastic photography and built on a trust-based relationship. Now, we call this conversational commerce, but to Georgia, it is the same sort of conversation you have going into a shop where they know you well, call you by your first name, and ask how you and the family are. She wanted the shopping experience to be a wonderful pleasure.

She used informative and inspirational images, and the conversational tone worked. The brand skyrocketed from the start. They often have a spare seat at the table for an imaginary person that speaks in their customers' shoes. They will ask what this customer representative would like or what they think about a particular suggestion. For example, when the Pantone colour of the year comes out, they will ask if "she" would have a bed in that colour. More often than not, the answer is no, but she agrees to try a cushion to show she is in fashion. So, they stock cushions, plus samples for anyone needing items for press shoots in this year's colour. Georgia also works hard to provide more than expected when it comes to delivery. It might be scented tissue paper or a surprise thank you gift after you have purchased a bed, but it always something that will surprise and delight.

Georgia quotes Warren Buffett saying, "It's only when the tide goes out that you learn who has been swimming naked." The trick is to keep ahead of the tide. Some large supplier brands refused to work with Georgia when she started because she didn't have a brick-and-mortar store, yet when COVID hit, the MD of one supplier came to her, telling her she was crushing it and asked what more they could do together. Georgia couldn't resist asking if it was no longer a concern that she didn't have a physical store. She has also turned down big names who are not a good fit for their brand, looking instead for shared values, excellent service, and unique products.

Georgia observes that although the experts say that multiple on-site pop-ups and address-capture work, she dislikes them when used too frequently. Georgia likens them to walking through Harrods and people leaping out at you spraying you with different perfumes. By the fourth one, you not only have lost interest in what you came to buy, but you are also no longer considering buying perfume.

Their current focus is on brand and product video content that provides valuable and informative content for customers. Georgia wants the experience to be frictionless and so enjoyable that customers will tell their friends, creating that tribe of fans to build the brand.

Customer experience

The sectors, the stories and the products are different but both Olly and Georgia use the art of communication to engage customers and deliver an experience they won't forget, because it is rooted in an emotional connection. It's all about communicating authentically in a way that ticks your customers emotional boxes.

CHAPTER TWENTY EIGHT

Selling and Pitching

Sales still exists, and it is an essential skill for many founders. This is particularly true in the B2B (business to business) world, but things have changed a great deal.

Of course, it is still vital that you measure your performance at every stage of the sales funnel, from first lead to sale, and indeed repeat sale. But what goes on within those processes has changed.

Smarketing

People are starting to talk about smarketing as if it is something new, when it is a phrase that has been around for over a decade, or nearer two decades, in some people's opinion. Smarketing is a place where marketing and sales meet on common ground for mutual benefit.

A middle ground is emerging, after marketing has attracted people to interact with the brand but before people are ready to be sold to: a relationship-building area that is still best managed under a sales leadership. But hard selling doesn't work anymore.

Sales exists mainly in B2B territory. Big contracts need personal handling, and research has become a considerable part of the job: researching the market, researching the prospect, and preparing the pitch. Good salespeople take much more time to do this preparation, resulting in fewer rejections, and delivering fewer pointless pitches.

Authenticity in sales

Professional business development has its heart in collaborations that benefit both parties. Yet sales still has this reputation for pushy people conning you into buying things you don't want.

Not doing the preparation and research is part of the reason. When I worked in telephone sales at the start of my career on short and horrendous contracts, we would be given lists of names and phone numbers with no other information and told to sell x product to these people. Small wonder that success was minimal.

Before even contacting anyone, you should know about the market, the company, what they do, the size of their market share, where they sit in the market, if they have a use for your product, and if their values match yours. As you get to know them, you can get to know those needs better and find out if that collaboration will be of genuine benefit.

Throughout, it is about developing an authentic relationship. My pet peeve is the salesperson calling you for the first time and launching with "how are you today." I know they don't care about the answer because they don't know me. So, what they have successfully achieved is to stick a great big fat label across their forehead that reads "insincere."

Avoid those pre-packaged ways to handle objections too. By those, I mean cringe-worthy openers, such as "if I could show you a way to make money/save money, increase your returns..." People aren't stupid, and they know they are being sold to, and barriers will be quickly raised. Instead, keep it honest, keep it authentic, and you will get on far better.

Initial appointments can be tough

When I was cornered into going on the road, back in my single-mum days, my car was old and needed to be parked where prospective customers would never see it. But as they also wanted to see samples, I had to lug tables or bedside cabinets down High Streets across the UK.

In those early days, I found it hard for another reason: we weren't all that good at what we did. Prospective buyers would find nail marks or blemishes and point them out, and I would be cringing and trying to hold my ground, saying blithely "obviously, these are only samples". Buyers would deliberately make it challenging for me. I remember one cobweb-filled back office that hadn't seen light for twenty-odd years. There, I was ordered to "stand over there in the corner and give us your speech". I had to climb over hazardous debris all over the floor to even to reach the corner.

One of my most nerve-wracking experiences was a few years in to that business when I was invited to pitch for a large contract of furniture sold through someone else's brand. As usual, I had arrived at the customer, a table in hand. The initial meeting was held in the company's showroom, a space so large that our factory would have fitted into it. Several senior executives were there, and the MD, who was not a small man, chose to sit on my table throughout the meeting. Every time he moved, I held my breath. There is nothing as distracting as having half your brain wondering if there will be an almighty crash as the table legs give way with my prospective customer crashing to the floor for an entire showroom full of people to see. Luckily the table held.

The markets aren't always ready

If you know about selling, you know about benefits and features and handling resistance. Lina Barker of Aaron Wallace, the grooming range for Black men, hit extraordinary resistance when she and Aaron first went out knocking on doors. They went out every day to hit Afro-Barbers' shops.

These shops are different from hair salons such as Toni and Guy's, which have an extensive retail section and generate a healthy proportion of profits from up-selling products. Aaron and Lina were keen to explain how this would be an excellent opportunity for the barbers' shops they were seeing, who at that point never had retail space for products of any sort. It was a good offer. They were offering a sale-or-return setup, so all the barbers' shops had to do was try it, pay for anything they sold and return the rest.

The majority said no. One or two reluctantly said yes, but when Lina and Aaron returned, there would be no sign of any products. Instead, they would be told that they were "in the back somewhere." What amazed Lina was that they were offering an opportunity for businesses to increase their revenue at no cost. You would think such an offer would be irresistible, yet the opposite was true.

Lina says most of these barbers are legacy businesses, with brilliant barbers who have never been interested in anything else. It is as far away as possible from the Toni-and-Guy-type culture, where every staff member is trained not just to cut hair but also on customer service and sales. These barbers saw it as too much effort and were too set in their ways to consider change. The pandemic forced Aaron Wallace online and colossal success followed, and Lina eventually started pitching to the giant retailers.

The Trust Factor

When Tim Mercer started Vapour, he began negotiating their first deal with a huge insurance company. Tim did have a sales background, but they were busy building a network, and without referrals from happy, satisfied customers to reassure potential buyers, it was challenging.

Tim says it came down to trust on both sides. He discovered they were willing to look at a smaller supplier because they thought they could get a more flexible, personal service than they would from one of the more prominent suppliers. They built trust and the company took a giant leap of faith.

Despite being the David pitching against Goliaths, Tim won another deal with Betfred, the vast betting chain. Tim heard that they wanted to change all their phone systems through a partner. Partly this was to introduce new, safer credit-card payment systems, where the person who works in the business never gets to hear the numbers. Betfred had a long-term contract with BT, but as sometimes happens with long-term contracts, no one had looked into Betfred's up-to-date needs.

Tim worked with them, found out their day-to-day challenges, and how they could save time, as well as add essential payment compliance. One business area was particularly sensitive, known in the betting industry as the "whales": customers who bet 50k and more on a single bet. Tim and his team developed a system that would recognize if one of the whales was calling and enable them to speak to the same customer-service person each time, even if they were at home and it was ten at night.

Increasingly, businesses need to develop this personal service for their clients. There are old school, big companies around that won't change because the costs would be too high, which open great sales opportunities for agile companies who listen and learn about their customers' needs. Great salespeople understand that while there may be a cheaper option, people are willing to pay more for personalized service, and that they can only deliver that by knowing what the customer needs.

Collaboration

You can learn all the fancy ways of handling objections, of noting your features, and highlighting your benefits. You can be Jerry McGuire on his best day at closing, but creating long-term relationships with customers demands more than that.

This means that you are putting together the best, most personalized proposition that works for both sides. Then everyone gets to win. And never forget to ask for recommendations and referrals, both of which are the lifeblood of growing sales.

CHAPTER TWENTY NINE

Customer Expectations

Business success follows customer happiness as surely as night follows day. But customer happiness isn't easy to achieve. We have to work hard at developing that circle, touching our customers' hearts, connecting with them and turning them into an army of fans that will not just keep buying, but will join the ranks of our best ambassadors.

However, the reality is that things do go wrong, sometimes horribly, and they can end up entirely out of our control. It takes a genuinely resilient leader and the right response to cope with disasters when the unexpected happens – that is what keeps customers on side.

When things go worse than you could have possibly imaged

The online learning platform Go1 is growing rapidly towards its goal of one billion learners worldwide. But early on, Andrew Barnes and his co-founders faced the same sort of challenges and heart-stopping moments most entrepreneurs do.

At one point, they had just won by far their most significant account, an entire country's civil service, which would bring in hundreds of thousands of users. It took Andrew and his co-founders several months to get ready, but finally, launch day arrived. Andrew flew in and was met by senior dignitaries for an official ribbon-cutting ceremony. Once the ribbon was cut, the new customers went to turn on the system, and the worst imaginable happened; it crashed.

The Go1 team had designed the system for that volume of users over a day, but not all at the same moment, which is what happened when everyone switched on for the opening ceremony. Andrew says he viscerally recalls thinking he had to immediately call an Uber, go to the airport and fly straight home.

Somehow, though, he managed not to allow himself to take that option. Instead, he suggested to his client that they go for lunch, and during that break, Andrew and his team managed to patch the system up sufficiently so that on their return, everything was working. This customer went on to be one of their best advocates. Andrew says he learned that is it is not what happens but how you deal with it that counts. People know that perfection is never possible.

Not Everyone is Understanding:

All of those who have been in business have battle stories to tell of skirmishes with unhappy customers. For example, Georgia Metcalfe of The French Bedroom Company related a horrendous episode, in which their credit provider declined to offer a potential customer credit. This customer reacted by announcing he was going to Uzi spray them. The team was somewhat shaken, so they all worked at home the next day, which was unknown to them at that time.

This aside, The French Bedroom Company retains its fantastic reputation through a combination of a strong brand and a fabulous customer experience. One example is how they arrange their own deliveries for the beds and take time to ask careful questions. These might range from finding out if their customer is expecting a baby, so might need the bed before a certain date, or if there are children in the house sleeping at particular times, so they can avoid disturbing them. They want to make it feel like you are having a gift delivered.

When things go wrong, Georgia says they have a toolbox of apologies to deliver if needed, from a handwritten letter of apology, to a free white-glove service (a premium delivery service), or occasionally even free bed linen. Georgia is also pragmatic. Because a wonderful bed is a once-in-a-lifetime purchase for most people, most of their customers are new. It costs £120 worth of google ads to find a new customer, so it has to be a viable balance. She is also fiercely protective of her customer-service team, who take up to two years to train fully, and are all emotionally intelligent with a deep sense of morality.

Service and Leadership in a crisis

The Suez Canal crisis in April 2021 brought Georgia some extreme customer service challenges. Goods on a French Bedroom Company container were stuck on the infamous "Ever Given" vessel, so they were impounded for insurance reasons. Georgia assembled all her department heads and put together a list of affected customers, some of whom were expecting their deliveries within two weeks. The sixty customers were divided into groups according to the severity and length of the delay. Every item of furniture on the container was handmade, and shipping containers were scarce during Covid, so the team knew that replacements would take up to nine months to make.

The senior team took the toughest, with Georgia personally called the worst impacted customers of all. She bought two enormous cakes, arranged a supply of tea, and then they all hit the phones, explaining what had happened and offering alternates. The calls went on late into the evening, as the only solution was a personal, empathetic, and genuine approach.

Out of the sixty customers they called, only one was unpleasant. A fellow business owner even sent Georgia's team a gift to congratulate them on how the crisis had been handled. It was a masterclass in how to turn a bad situation into a winning one.

Champagne, Love and Human Connection

For years, Charlotte Pearce and her company Inkpact have been having constant conversations about human connection. Making people feel significant, thought of and wowing people are at the heart of what they do.

They send genuinely handwritten notes, at scale, for big brands like John Lewis, BrewDog, L'Occitane and Sweaty Betty. They regularly get feedback that customers loved their notes, or that they made their day or made them cry. They are kept on mantlepieces and shared on social media.

Customers take the notes into stores to say thank you or, most commonly, do the lick test, where they lick their finger to check that the note is genuinely handwritten. When it smudges, people are astounded that a big company wrote to them by hand. But recently, Charlotte heard a story that made her giggle about a new level of lick test.

A customer of a well-known retailer wrote in after receiving her handwritten, thank you note. The customer explained how much she loved her note, relaying that when she showed it to her husband, he said, "It's lovely, but how much of my money do you spend there to get that?" To check it was real, she took out her champagne (as you do) and used it to see if the ink smudged. It did, and she was so delighted she wrote to the company to tell them that the champagne test worked.

Charlotte says that this story highlights a few things about which she says she has been chewing people's ears off for years. When you do something thoughtful, memorable, and treat people like humans, it is more impactful than anything else. Customers then react with loyalty. Charlotte explains that you simply can't get a story or reaction like this with a mass-marketed, quick-win email. When you make your customers feel significant, they will act significantly, and you will have both a lifelong customer and a meaningful relationship with them. Business relationships are not as different from personal relationships as we think. One tip Charlotte gives is that if you keep behaving like you did at the beginning of a relationship, the relationship goes from strength to strength.

Customer relations summed up

These three stories explain what customer service is all about: continually working on connecting with your customers on a personal, human and emotional level, going above and beyond, not panicking in a crisis, but squaring your shoulders and working through it - and making every customer know that they personally matter. Above all, look after yourself and your customer-service people. It is a job that can take its toll.

Who Is With You On The Journey

You are only ever going to be as good as your team. Great leaders make great teams, teams that love to work with them. To become a great leader you will need all that self-development time we talked about earlier in the book.

You need to find passion, be crystal clear in your direction, be inspirational in your vision, connect with the team, and then get out of their way and let them do their job. And when we talk about vision, remember it isn't making a hundred nuts and bolts a day at x profit – it is about the impact: the people you will affect by doing it.

Finding the right people is hard, and keeping them is even harder. There are many different aspects of culture, so in this section we will look at how to ensure people thrive and are happy, how to encourage innovation, and how to maintain a particular culture even if you are running a remote business. What is also increasingly important is offering people training and development that matches their individual goals in life.

Be wary of how easy it is to sacrifice culture for growth. Grow too fast in one hit, and your start-up culture is often the sacrificial lamb. Make the office your team's second home, or better still, let your people make it their second home. Build the culture from the top, making people feel secure and worthwhile, and add people who will continue building the culture. Encourage your team to bond in every way you can, at work and outside work. And trust them.

CHAPTER THIRTY

Forming a Senior Management Team

For a business to grow sustainably, a senior team has to be capable and willing to grow alongside it. For founders, hiring the right senior people often means stepping outside our comfort zone because our natural inclination is to hire people we trust, often family or friends, and put that above the skill sets that we need. We are also drawn to hiring people similar to ourselves, especially when we are exhausted and overworked. So, we grab onto the first person we see who can do some of what we do in the same way we do. These approaches don't work.

The Benefits of Experience

If this is your first-time scaling, what you are lacking is experience. So, to optimize your business, you need to take a long hard look at yourself and decide where your weaknesses lie. For example, are you a poor people person, do you lack knowledge in scaling, do you lack operations experience? Another great question to ask when looking at people comes from the founders of Stripe, who would ask "Could I see myself working for you?"

The next challenge is where to find these gems. Phenomenally successful serial entrepreneur Chad Wasilenkoff, currently the founder of Helicoid Industries, says that finding the right people is far easier when you know your sector. That knowledge gives you a much greater chance of attracting the best talent.

Many start-ups fail because they run out of cash, and Chad says this is another area in which an experienced team is a massive plus. They will help prevent that, forecast, and see nuances that you might not yet have the experience to spot. In the worst-case scenario, they will also see when something is not going to work quicker than you will. While that might bring grief, sooner is always better than later. Chad believes that world class talent saves money in the long run. Exceptional people will still be hungry to learn and grow further alongside the business.

Top-calibre people are only going to be attracted by big dreams. Chad describes it as avoiding talking about the perfect hamburger stall if you want investment to go into the restaurant trade. If you map out your plans for a global chain, you might see ears pricking up. Chad adds that once you have a senior management team, the next challenge is to get out of their way, not second guess them.

Play to your strengths, hire for your weaknesses

Vicky Whiter moved from the corporate world to entrepreneurship. Having acquired Peters' Cleaners, before she knew it, she was pitching to investors with a disruptive business plan to change the local stores into unmanned pods at busy railway stations. She had also acquired a senior team to form her board for the future.

Vicky says that all start-ups need good advice in the beginning, exactly when they don't have the money for it. Vicky often turns to her father, who also used to be an entrepreneur and angel, having been Founder and Chairman of, amongst others, a company with a similar business model, Coffee Nation.

Two others complete her board. When Vicky first pitched to investors, she understood that she didn't have the marketing knowledge to bring her vision to life. Vicky recruited Clare Gill via LinkedIn. Clare's background was working at a high level for Morrison's supermarkets. Vicky was nervous that Clare might not be happy coming from such a senior position to end up doing all aspects of marketing, but Clare relishes the idea of being a part of creating something new from the bottom up. Vicky admits few entrepreneurs are methodical, whereas Clare was brilliant at methodical work.

The second person was an investor Vicky met through fund-raising. Andy brings financial expertise, has also been an MD of a vending company, and has some experience of franchises. He can produce figures to win instant credibility and confidence with other investors. In addition, Andy can run the data-driven side of their marketing analysis. At the moment, he has equity, but as the company can afford it, he will become an official non-executive director.

All three come from professional backgrounds, which provides common ground. But it is also the perfect formation of an early senior team because Vicky has balanced her own strengths and weaknesses, finding people that – together – will make up a complete package. New founders sometimes assume their "little start-up idea" would never be of interest to people coming from big corporation, but the truth is that great people are often looking for exciting opportunities where their contribution can make a difference.

Building a high-quality team from start-up

Some founders resist bringing in high-quality people early on. I think there are a variety of reasons. They think it will cost too much or believe that no one that good would consider joining them. Sometimes, they are afraid of people with more knowledge and experience.

The reality is that you cannot grow indefinitely without a management team, so getting quality people on board may as well be a problem you face up to early on. The better the quality of your people, the faster you will grow. There is also the old adage that you are the sum of the five people closest to you (Jim Rohn), so who you hire will also impact your personal development. Instead of viewing it as something to worry over, look at it as an exciting opportunity. Additionally, you will be able to off-load work in the areas that you don't excel in and concentrate more on what you do best. The chances are high that what you do best is what you enjoy most.

This brings us to how start-ups can attract quality people and where you find them. Once you are successful, it becomes far easier to attract high-quality people. They are attracted by that success, the customer base, the product, and above all, the vision. But in the early days, you are entirely reliant on your vision and how inspiring you can make it.

Pitching to potential early management is much the same as pitching to investors. They are potentially looking to invest their time at well under the market rate, so they have to be both excited and committed about the prospect of doing so. I spoke to one entrepreneur in the States who demonstrated potential with a slide of their target clients, who were massive global names. Such was the power of this vision, combined with his absolute conviction, he was able to recruit his early team even before he had managed to get a single customer on board.

Recruitment companies are beyond the resources of most start-ups. Therefore, word of mouth is the way forward. Another advantage of such a personal way of recruiting is that it helps address the trust issue surrounding handover, which often looms large in the founder's mind at that point. Later on, head-hunters can be sent out to look for the cream of the crop of talent, but for now, that is not the way to go.

For the early management team, relevant experience is critical so put feelers out within your sector. However, experience alone is not the only thing you need. You want to identify people keen to learn and grow with the company. Someone who wants to do everything the way they have always done it will stultify your team. I made the error of hiring a couple of those myself. They had vast industry experience, but were completely unable to adapt to new ways, were stunned at having to work in an open office or not having a secretary, and struggled to adapt to novel procedures. They need to be humble enough to muck in and make the tea to start with, yet able to grow and become leaders in their own right, eventually becoming able to push the company through to the next level.

Cultural fit is also absolutely crucial. As you grow, your new management will build teams of their own, and each team will need to be developed as a cohesive part of the whole.

Above all, they need to be hugely excited about the vision. The level of people you want will crave something new to build and be so excited by the picture of where the company is going and why that they will be open to earning, at least in part, through equity.

The Benefits of Equity Sharing

A wide variety of equity management schemes offer share schemes specifically for employees, particularly management, at a level that will grow with the company. Relationships are immediately transformed, gaining loyalty, advocacy, commitment, and capability. Equity sharing doesn't just result in an ownership mindset and an immediate improvement in performance, it also encourages decision-making for the benefit of the company rather than the individual. Share schemes create advocates within the company and push forward a culture of success.

The schemes themselves vary. People were wary about giving away equity in the past, but many of the issues have now been eradicated. If people fail to achieve, options are built to protect the founder and company, and equity is released only when commitments are fully met. Schemes can be reversible, which is very different and much safer for founders than it used to be.

Giving away a bit of your baby

Giving away bits of your company often becomes a stumbling block in founders' minds. Despite this, share schemes and equity management for staff at various levels have become much more popular. With part ownership, people have more say in their own future, and in return, the company can access more talent than they could otherwise afford.

If you want to go this route, use specialist advisors. Sharing equity is a complex, specialized business that, done wrong, could reduce your company's value and leave you unprotected with unfair conditions on both sides. The initial outlay to a professional firm will protect you and your company.

Shared equity at any level can positively impact performance, loyalty and culture – in addition to cash flow. For your senior team, it means a direct interest in the business's success and a share in the long-term rewards – and that massively increases your chances of attracting the high-quality people you will need from the start.

CHAPTER THIRTY ONE

Hiring for Growth

When I ask recruitment companies about finding hires for entrepreneurial companies, they either say they don't cover that market, or that recruitment should be the same as for any other company. I disagree. The two worlds are entirely different.

Within corporates, recruitment by skills alone is often encouraged. They also have sufficient staff to avoid panic hiring. Firefighting recruiting is the Achilles heel of entrepreneurial companies, that with eyes focused firmly on the purse strings, only recruit when it becomes essential, which is far too late.

Panic hires rarely end well. The lack of cultural fit can be overlooked, with key questions skipped over and niggling voices ignored. Carefully thought out, detailed questions about tasks that the applicant would have carried out previously, why they made the choices they did and what they achieved are glossed over. In the rush, asking for references is often skipped too. This is usually the result of a combination of faith in the gut, and a shortage of time, which can lead to hugely expensive mistakes.

One approach to help prevent this and strengthen culture is to let the team be a part of the final decision. Several successful companies talk loudly about "keeping the idiots out" or similar phrases. What that really means is keeping out people who wouldn't fit with the own existing culture, which is perfect from an HR perspective.

While corporates may be predominantly focused on aptitude and skill matching, entrepreneurs focus on a mix of these plus the way that a potential employee's values fit with those of the company: flexibility, desire, and the ability to self-develop. A match in beliefs is crucial to building a robust and cohesive culture.

Culture starts with your recruitment

Dr Jeff Chen, MD, MBA, describes himself as a rebel with a cause. He is the CEO and co-founder of Radicle Science, a California company revolutionizing the clinical validation of non-prescription, natural health products. Radicle recently completed the largest randomized trial of CBD ever conducted.

Antarctic explorer Ernest Shackleton is one of Jeff's greatest inspirations, especially since he too is navigating completely uncharted waters. Since Radicle is very much a rebellion against the institutional status quo, bringing on people with a rebel's heart has been an imperative part of their hiring process and company culture.

When it came to hiring their first employees, Jeff remembered Shackleton's advertisement for his expedition, which read "Men Wanted: for hazardous journey, small wages, bitter cold, long months of complete darkness, constant danger, safe return doubtful, honour and recognition in case of success."

Jeff paraphrased his own version: "The work will be hard, and safety is not guaranteed, but if we succeed, we will permanently alter the course of medicine for all future generations."

When Emily Pauli saw the ad, she exclaimed, "I think I've found my people!" She is now Radicle Science's Chief Research Officer, and blazing a new trail in revolutionizing healthcare.

Using Values to Recruit

Daniel Koffler is the founder of the New-York-City-based New Frontiers Executive Function. They work with both individuals and groups in organizational and academic settings through periods of transition, starting with a deeply ingrained belief that society at large doesn't prepare us for life's challenges and experiences, and that leaves particular groups of people significantly disadvantaged.

Daniel readily admits that they didn't have a formalized culture for many years. He had a sense of what he wanted the company to feel and behave like, based around the "do unto others as you wish others to do unto you" principle, but it was never formalized on paper or spoken of, and therefore never used in decision-making or recruitment. Team members interpreted it in their individual ways. Looking back, Daniel can see that almost all the problems they had related to them flying blind on core values. He says they got "lucky" with a few key hires who now drive the business forward, but others didn't work out, and he had to go through the painful process of letting them go, before having to re-hire, re-train and re-integrate new employees. Each time it happened, it wasted precious energy and resources.

They had continual problems revolving around hiring and team building. On one occasion, they justified bringing in someone with a very different style because they had the skill sets the company needed and imagined that the challenge might cause them to be less reliant on assumptions. It led to immense friction. The team made every attempt to accommodate this individual, even experimenting with changes to their own proven approaches. These efforts led to recriminations and the need for significantly more administrative time, energy, and money. Not only was the new hire unproductive, but they were also a bad fit, and the theory that the different styles would mix things up produced disastrous consequences. Daniel says that while it is always painful to exit someone, what was needed was to change the new hire's personality, which was not fair on the individual or the organization. The experience taught them a lot.

Daniel admits he had always thought values to be a very "crunchy" concept that had nothing to do with the P & L. However, he changed his mind when he found the EOS concept, a business management system that takes people, processes, and profit into account. They had numerous brainstorming sessions with key people and other team members, deciding what defined them. They looked at the team's best members, asked both what makes them the best, and imagined what a whole company like them could achieve.

The values they settled on were Accountability, Empathy, Creativity, Integrity, Personal Development, and Authenticity. They are a collection of themes that they feel best represents who they are, who they want to be, and who they want to work/align themselves with. It took time, not just to define them, but also to understand what it meant to be very intentional and thoughtful about the values. There was confusion when determining them, followed by disagreement and some emotional interactions. Eventually, the group became so tired that they settled on a batch of values initially that were not as thoughtful as they should have been. But they dug deeper, justified each one, and now they use them as the criteria to choose who they work with and employ.

Daniel learned that culture is king, and if changes need to be made, the sooner you do so, the better. Untangling takes far longer. It takes leadership from the top to achieve and will lead to pushback and discomfort, but the results are incredible. From the point they agreed on their values, New Frontiers experienced a 48% increase year on year. But as importantly, it is the quality of their business, who they work with, how they work, and what they do in terms of exceeding both staff and customer expectations that has improved beyond expectation.

Innovation in recruitment

Deepak Shukla, founder of the Pearl Lemon Group, is one of many entrepreneurs who are now drawing on global talent for growth. With a rapidly growing team, he has learned to take innovative approaches. He started to question the stereotypical story that you cannot find the talent you need in developing countries and deliberately tested the data to see if there was any truth in it. Deepak found it to be inaccurate.

He finds terrific talent in The Philippines, India, and Uganda, and follows the same strict hiring processes as anywhere else. He says you have to be realistic and view it as a numbers game when recruiting. He also says to use a very job-functional, specific recruitment process that identifies the uncut diamond: talent that hasn't been allowed to shine so far. His recruits come with perseverance, resilience, and a great work ethic combined with a determination to be part of a company in the west, and often end up outperforming their western colleagues.

Deepak has an equally innovative approach when it comes to hiring salespeople. Good salespeople are challenging to find. Too often, there was a gap between what they could do and what they said they could do. While Deepak understood they needed self-belief, all too often, it translated into overselling and under-performing combined with an unrealistic salary expectation. Deepak asked himself where he could find the talented people he needed to make sales from outside the industry, to talk on the phone, present well and build relationships.

Sales and theatre people have been linked for many generations. At some stage, even the old sales interview question "I am Will Shakespeare, so sell me this pen" spilled back into drama schools. Deepak had done GCSE drama, but also tried his hand at rapping in his 20s, and could see that being on screen and performing were similar to the skillset needed for sales.

Deepak now lists sales positions on a casting platform and job board for aspiring and existing performers, musical or theatre, or anyone presenting themselves to the world at large. When using more traditional portals such as LinkedIn, he states that applicants with performing experience will be preferred. He says that the result is a wonderful world of performers who don't oversell themselves as salespeople often do. There is a humility and earnestness about the performance skills, combined with an ability to connect by adjusting different mindsets, vocabularies, and tones dependent on the scenario. These people make up some of his very best salespeople.

Ability to Develop

The good news is that working for a start-up has become not just acceptable but trendy. The Great Resignation is partly because the trust level in big corporates is low, and opportunity is now seen to be with the ever-growing numbers of start-ups. But not every candidate is suited to it. An employee's role will be defined in detail within a large company, and they will not be asked to step outside it, which some people like.

Within a start-up, everyone knows what is going on, and

everyone is expected to be a team player, leaping in no matter what needs doing, and fast. It is that willingness to adapt, to contribute, that you need most and is often the hardest personality trait to find. Skill sets can be taught.

Australian entrepreneur Matt Bullock has built two software companies and, in the process, refined precisely what he needs when recruiting. People need to be willing to put in what Matt describes as "stupid effort." He has two key interview questions, asking "Do you want to go fast?" and "Do you want to change?" The answers help Matt to find people who will cope with what is needed in an entrepreneurial company. Many cannot.

Hiring for growth means nailing the culture, being innovative about where you look, and looking for people that relish the challenge of getting outside their comfort zones and developing alongside the company.

CHAPTER THIRTY TWO

Culture for Happiness

Company culture is the pixie dust of entrepreneurship. A strong, cohesive culture that everyone wants to belong to is almost unbeatable. And most start-ups have the real thing, even without realizing it. Everyone is excited, fired up by the vision, loving being a part of the journey. Founders know every team member well and take a genuine interest in that person, their hopes, fears, families. The word that comes up the most is "fun".

Things change as companies grow, even at the stage of having just six to twelve people. It is no longer possible or practical for everyone to know all the details of every job and every customer. Projects and workload have to get a little more broken up. Meanwhile, the founders are becoming overloaded elsewhere, from hiring to strategy to fund-raising, and the key components of culture can get lost. Sadly, stories of poor culture are all too familiar, but this one has to be one of the worst.

Ever taken a gun to work?

One contact of mine worked for a company with a brilliant CEO, a clever man, a great guy to have a pint with but 'way out there'. On my contact's very first day, this man smashed a Macbook and threw it at the head of one of his employees.

It was usual to hear him shouting from down in the street. He fired his whole marketing department for poor performance, then complained that no one was doing any marketing and hired them again, only to repeat the same firing and re-hiring process a few months later.

A CEO's style sets the style of the whole culture. Because this particular leader was aggressive, so were all the senior management. Many of the senior team were taking anti-depressants. It became so bad that someone there brought a gun to the office to shoot their manager. It was a horrendously toxic company with one of the highest attrition rates my contact had ever seen. Extreme culture nearly always filters down from the top.

Leadership

HR and Health and Safety companies' briefs are to minimize litigation and take over some of the duties of the overworked founder. Too often, this translates into minutely detailed, crystal-clear job descriptions, and rules and regulations that are all highly detrimental to culture. What it delivers is accountability and control with a large tablespoon of micromanaging and fear for good measure. The team then becomes distant from customer needs and resentful of both founder and company, and in turn, the founder becomes distant from the group. Everyone loses.

Culture comes from the top and it is your vision and commitment to your team and their shared values that will make them happy. That mission can never get lost. Connection is crucial. Your job as a leader is to communicate that vision regularly, be continually honest with your team, and ensure they see and receive the benefits of what they do along the way.

Vision, Values, and People who fit

Within many immensely successful tech companies, the word fun makes a regular appearance in their cultural ethos. The principle is simple: happy people having fun achieve better results.

To ensure a strong culture is maintained, recruitment has to be careful, and very culture focussed. Cultural fit is at the forefront when it comes to recruiting but it doesn't stop there. A strong and in-depth on-boarding process follows and that concentrates on embedding the values and culture. Some companies are so passionate about the importance of preserving cultural fit, that at the end of their in-boarding period, they will offer a pay-off to anyone who is a bad fit. The benefits are two-fold. There is less fear of being fired, and the cost is cheaper than keeping someone who could damage the successful culture.

Culture plays a massive role in why people stay in their jobs and therefore in companies achieving good retention. The more definitive the culture, the more precise the fit. Sometimes the definition may divide people, but that is precisely why it works. The clearer the culture is, the more evident to everyone involved if someone fits – or not.

Retention starts before each new person joins you. They should already have been emailed the mission and values, along with a personal welcome letter from the founder. The more welcome you make them feel, the more they will be sure that they belong. Their on-boarding week should be joyous and let them know that they belong.

Extreme rotten-apple hires often sneak in when you are panic-hiring during growth, desperate for the skill set, and end up succumbing to someone who appears to say and do all the right things. A rotten apple is someone who may well be good at the job, and popular with the team but who subtly undermines the culture at every opportunity. Someone working against you on the inside can turn your culture from good to poisonously toxic and, in extreme cases, wreck a business or a reputation. Never panic hire! And if you sense the culture changing, take action – fast. Trust your gut.

Micro-Managing never works:

Dr Craig Knight is an occupational psychologist and founder of Identity Realization. Craig sums up successful culture as happy people performing at their best, staying longer, and says that this is achieved in a few important ways.

The first is to allow people to feel part of a team they naturally gravitate to, not one that is chosen for them, so that they truly belong. The second is to ensure that employees have autonomy over when they do their work. The third is to purge any micro-management. The more autonomy people have, and the more trust they are given to do (and resources to complete) the job for which they were employed, the happier they will be. People who are engaged with an organization tend to buy into its vision and accept its goals. Good management means letting go.

Craig has come across some horrendous examples of over-controlling management. At one particular company, supervision by junior managers included monitoring which websites people visited; even keystrokes were monitored, along with bathroom breaks, which, if too frequent, were subject to investigation.

Craig says the extraordinary thing about this sort of monitoring is that it only happens to the more junior staff. He recalls listening to the ex-MP Steven Norris talk at a conference where one company was being feted. Mr Norris asked the management if they monitored all the calls and internet usage of their staff, to which the answer was yes. He then asked the senior manager if he was also subjected to the same scrutiny. Of course, he was not. Craig points out that the irony is that lower down the food chain, people are unlikely to make errors of any significance, whereas, at senior management level, the impact can be huge. We monitor junior staff, to the detriment of both mental well-being and performance, yet trust managers to operate without any such constraints.

The environment also matters enormously. When people work in an office, tidiness and regimentation are often part of the dictate, though are rarely conducive to productivity despite being the leitmotif of management control. Craig advocates giving control of the workplace to the people at work in the workplace.

Retention of staff depends more than a little on trust. It isn't about control, but creating mutual boundaries, about letting go, so people want to stay and spend time with you.

Ownership Culture

When leaders continually link what is getting done to the vision, everyone starts thinking like this. If your people buy in, and you let go, they develop a natural sense of responsibility and desire to contribute their part towards the vision. Ego goes out the window. High performers are valued by the people that matter: other team members. It is part of what Craig was describing: ownership culture.

People don't just want a job. They want more work-life balance, more choice as to when and where they work, and more purpose in what they do. Meanwhile, leaders are free to find out what each of their team wants to achieve and ensure that it happens, so people grow alongside the company.

In a company with an ownership culture, employees genuinely feel they have a stake in the organization, and this approach is proven to reap rewards. Meetings with management become positive, and ideas and excitement about where everyone is going and its impact are shared. Goals are agreed jointly, and management is there to support if needed.

Ownership culture is built on trust, honesty, transparency, humanity, connecting as human beings, and working together towards the vision.

CHAPTER THIRTY THREE

A Culture of Innovation

O ne of the traits that most successful companies have in common is an innovative culture. To pin down what that means, it is a culture where everyone involved works towards continually improving the company in every way. That may sound obvious, and to some extent, it is, but it also requires people who are comfortable with innovating and developing. It is certainly more usual in the start-up phase, when everyone is focused on making something great. But, as with a good culture, innovation also – all too often – disappears as companies grow.

Part of the reason for that is simply that not everyone is comfortable pushing hard all the time, especially outside their comfort zone. Indeed, some people actively dislike this type of culture. As you grow, it becomes increasingly hard to only hire people who do enjoy it. Remember Matt Bullock's two hiring questions.

Companies have to have innovation deeply embedded into their culture to achieve it. Elon Musk's companies, well known for innovation, see it as critical to success. They are aggressive in their encouragement, with rewards for innovation and big penalties for failure to innovate. People are constantly encouraged to share their ideas, their suggestions for innovation. People are pushed to their limits, and some wither under that pressure. I got advice from an expert.

Innovation can be scary.

Michael Holmstrom is known for his ground-breaking work in STEM education with his company STEM Punks. Originally from Sweden, Michael has had several companies, including a consultancy specializing in implementing digitally-enabled strategies and running Enterprise Workshops aiming to harness the power of innovation.

Michael says he has learned that there is a great deal more to success than having a degree. It requires relating to people, understanding different cultures, and problem-solving. Every company wants people to be innovative. It is often the topic of the first question in a job interview, but creating an entire innovative culture is very different from talking about it and not easy to achieve.

Michael grew up in Sweden. He would spend his time in the garage tinkering in the short days and long, dark nights. In the garage, Michael worked out how to make things, from a massive tree-cutting tool to converting his first bike into a faster, electric one. He came to realize that he wanted to be an engineer, and won a place at university, the first in his family to do so.

The garage was the perfect place to foster innovation. The crucial lesson Michael learned was that failure led to success, and the garage felt a safe place to fail. People who succeed big always suffer plenty of failures, but it doesn't matter, because they are not afraid of them. Michael says there is no shortage of good ideas but a shortage of people who can create value from them.

What stops people from innovating is two things: the first is that fear of failure we discussed earlier. We are programmed from school onwards to avoid people laughing at us. Second is the fear of rejection. Whenever we first experience it, from our parents, at school, or in our first relationships, we discover that it's horrible. So, we stay safe and don't risk it. Yet it is people who cope well with rejection that succeed in life. Take any good salesman; they will hear the word 'no' a hundred times a day, but will still think it is the best day ever when they break the pattern and make a sale. They accept failure is part of the journey to success.

Young children learn everything from trial and error and still know how to innovate. Teaching them is easy. Michael says that by the time we get to the boardroom, fear of rejection makes cultural innovation incredibly hard. The bigger a company gets, the harder it becomes; the older people are, the harder it is to teach them. To break down those barriers, Michael always starts with a problem and explains how to achieve an innovation mindset.

Repackaging change and innovation

Relevance is also part of the secret. You need to grab people's attention with something so interesting that they forget the fear. Michael says that if he runs an after-school coding class, it will always attract the same people. However, if he asks people to join a group to find solutions to supplying clean water in Ghana, he will immediately get a cross-section of people interested in the environment or helping others. People stop worrying if they have the skills or ability when they are focused on a problem.

With kids, presenting a problem they want to solve makes learning easy. With adults, a lot of change management is needed, especially when it comes to innovation or getting people's heads around tech. For example, STEM Punks had a contract with a vast mining firm in Australia to re-train the traditional workforce, truck drivers, and digger drivers when all the vehicles were becoming automated. People's minds were closed. Their natural inclination was that they couldn't ever understand tech and robotics and were convinced they would fail. Michael used the same model of presenting problems that needed solving to completely distract from the skills issue and get people interested and inspired.

The importance of trust

Opening minds and encouraging innovation starts with building trust. Michael also works with abused kids and he recently ran a three-day innovation class. They all came in, hoods pulled forward, not meeting each other's eyes, saying nothing. Michael created the same environment as in his garage in Sweden, one of mutual respect, with nothing to fear in failure, and opportunities to learn on their own terms. By the end of day two, the hoods were off, and they were engaging with each other and creating amazing things. When you have trust, that risk of failure isn't scary anymore.

Entrepreneurship is about 90% failure, so you have to get past that to be successful. At least half the stuff you do may be complete rubbish, but by doing a lot, you start to learn how to do something high value. Entrepreneurship takes persistence, strategy, and fast validation.

It is the same with creating innovative teams that can adapt to new things. Tech and STEM are just tools; it is the open mindset and desire for problem solving that needs to be created. To create innovative teams, you must give people that safe environment where they can fail fast, learn by doing, and have no mental blocks distracting them.

Michael challenges people to start each new day doing something deliberately that they will fail at, and to embrace that feeling because it is the first step towards innovation and creativity. We can solve problems by creating people who can transform ideas into value.

Trying is valued, failure accepted.

Innovation has to be embedded into company culture by everyone being involved, encouraged and rewarded when they contribute ideas, even if they are unsuccessful. The key to an innovative business is to promote innovation and creativity at every single level because it is innovators who can identify which ideas could be successful and how that can happen at a viable economic cost.

Innovation can be a series of small changes or one large one. But wherever it appears, it is at the heart of business success. Businesses that continually innovate will be more competitive, more efficient, and build their value. As a result, the companies that don't do it stagnate and end up at risk from the competition.

To increase profits, you might want to radically change your service or product, or automate some parts, for example. You might be overhauling and re-assessing your pricing structure in the hope of seeing a significant increase in revenue. You may want to improve products and services, but also introduce new ones. You may be expanding into a completely new field or new sector. All of these strategies need innovation.

Finding ways your business could innovate always starts with research to establish the problem. You need to understand where you stand in the marketplace, your strengths, and your weaknesses. You need to understand your customer's needs, what they are looking for but not getting from anyone in the market. Ideally, part of your time or business's resources, depending on the size of your business, should be continually allocated to researching trends and spotting opportunities, checking the competition, and beating them at their own game. You can use the internet, talk to your suppliers, and above all, talk to your customers. An innovative culture means that you and your team will thrive on coming up with solutions to any challenges that arise.

CHAPTER THIRTY FOUR

Remote Cultures

The pandemic flung companies who had never considered home working into disarray. They quickly discovered that running a team remotely is very different from in the office. However, when people are working at home, micro-management is just as disastrous as it is in the office – if not more so. People had to flex their work round their home commitments. Managers accustomed to assessing output in hours worked had to scramble to learn the art of results-based managing. But perhaps the biggest challenge for "newbie" remote managers was how to foster the strong culture that they used to achieve in the office. Of course, it was easier for people who already had a strong remote culture before lockdown.

Not the army as you know it

Tim Mercer had been in the armed forces, spending his 18th birthday as a soldier in Northern Ireland and his 21st in Iraq. A successful career in sales followed, but when Tim saw a market opportunity for a new cloud tech business, he sold everything – from the family home to his wife's car. He set up Vapour in 2013.

Tim says that his leadership style comes from his army days but that the perception of the armed forces is skewed. People believe that you get shouted at and do as you are told. The reality, if your life is on the line, is that you need to speak up and contribute to the plan to give it every chance of success. So, within Vapour, he tells everyone where the business needs to go, and everyone is encouraged to contribute to the discussion, say so if they don't like it, and add to the plan. But once the talks are over, they have had their chance, and everyone gets on with it.

When Tim started, he knew the ideal person to do everything he hated, the systems, operations and processes, having worked with her previously. However, his former colleague, Carol McGrotty lived in Glasgow and told him that on no account was she moving. So unusually, for back then, Tim set up the business with everyone working remotely. The systems that they needed to do that worked because Carol made them work.

Both went to a course at the Cambridge Business School, and there Tim had what he says is some of the most valuable feedback he had ever received. They told him that when planning things from 1 to 10, he starts at 7. Most people are still at points 1 or 2 in the thought process, which is why they can't keep up or follow him. This lesson taught him to discuss things early in the process.

Tim says that some people are more challenging to bond together into a team atmosphere. But he actively looks for people who bond, and to strengthen that they get together remotely once or twice a week. The tone is deliberately jolly, not too serious, and the question of how best to look after the customer is always at the forefront of discussions.

Then once a month, they get together in person for a catch-up of some sort. Sometimes this is for a more formal event to raise money for charity, sometimes for a drink or dinner. Tim says some people say they can't do it because they have children, dogs or cats, and he always tells them to bring them too. The secret lies in being flexible and making people feel wanted.

The argument for a Hybrid Model

As the pandemic progressed, I saw some friends flourish working remotely and others wilt, hating their enforced separation from teammates and the camaraderie that goes with it. I have come to the simple conclusion that because we humans are all different, there isn't a one-size-fits-all solution for every company.

Most companies were faced with adapting to remote working at the start of the pandemic. The biggest challenge that founders reported was the loss of culture. But that is being solved by innovative leaders and many people have come to prefer working from home, at least part of the time. When people have the choice of where and how they work, then recruitment and retention become easier. They can also reduce their carbon footprint and, for many, their stress levels.

In recognition of this, many companies are going hybrid, and some, such as 3M, offer a mix. HubSpot is another example. People can be office-based three or more days a week, flexible, in the office two days or less a week, or entirely home working. They can change their choice once a year.

It adds enormous challenges to management. Not only do you have all the issues over trust, the change to results-based outcomes, and the need to find the right tech that works for you and suits your culture and team, but you also have specific hybrid challenges to look out for.

The first is inclusiveness and lack of bias. The more you see people, the easier it is to bond, but the company cannot, in any way, favour one person – for example – who comes into the office three days a week over someone who works at home.

If you are retaining office space and, therefore, the overheads, you have other considerations. For example, you might be able to manage with less space or get by sharing it with someone else. But more than that, you have to design it intentionally to meet the needs of people coming to the office. You might well be providing meeting rooms, therefore, and almost certainly both collaboration and social spaces. Everywhere needs to be linked to everyone – wherever they are.

In my early working years, I often took on home working jobs. This was a long time before culture was considered relevant in any way. I wasn't very good at my job, and not through lack of capability, necessarily. I had a working target quota, but it meant nothing to me and had no relation to my own goals. I had no idea what the company's aims were, didn't identify with them and didn't know anyone else at the company. Not surprisingly, I didn't give a hoot about the results.

Now that home working and hybrid working are here to stay, everything you do has to be to re-enforce culture and connection. Intentional planning and leadership to give people that sense of purpose and belonging and making what everything going on relevant to them personally is crucial.

Culture across continents

If you think remote and hybrid culture is challenging, think of the challenge of running companies worldwide and across very different cultures. Craig Dempsey is co-founder of BLH Group, a back-office services provider mainly focused on Latin America and the Caribbean. He is from Australia, and they also do business there and in New Zealand. As an ex-military vet and former mining executive, Craig has had experience in some of these countries. However, the company has grown since its inception in 2014, from having a single office in Colombia, to having offices in sixteen countries around Latin America and the Caribbean, which bring a headache-inducing amount of complexity.

As with every continent, there are communications issues in Latin America, not just surrounding foreigners coming into the region speaking pigeon Spanish or Portuguese but also with the native Spanish. Meanings of words change between countries. Craig moves between seventeen major cities and says he has learned, often the hard way, how bad this can be. It might be funny looking back, but you run the very real risk of upsetting people.

For example, in Colombia, chicha means bad armpit odour, while in Chile, it means something far away, and in Argentina, it's slang for the female private parts. If you have been to some Latin American countries, you might have ordered cake (torta), but if you place the same order in Mexico, you could get a sandwich. No wonder confusion and potentially, offence can arise.

Similar problems occur when talking business: timing is one example. If you tell someone from Chile that something is happening "a hora", that means "right now". In Colombia, meanwhile, it means "sometime relatively soon" (in Colombia, "yam" means "right now"). Similarly, "un rate" might be a long or short period of time, depending on where you are. Even a good grasp of Spanish doesn't save you from error.

With years of experience now under his belt, Craig can help bridge the cultural gap for their clients, having seen – and experienced – the pitfalls for himself.

Hybrid, Remote, Cross continental

If your team is remote, hybrid, or stretched over several continents, it all comes down to that magic word, communication. It is a question of working out what suits your business, your team, sector, and way of working – and amplifying that communication to fit. And devoting a lot of time and energy to developing culture, wherever your teams are.

CHAPTER THIRTY FIVE

Learning and Development

Finding and hiring the right people is getting increasingly more challenging, and as we have seen, means putting culture first and skills second. So, training existing team members can seem like a solution when you need people with a more developed skill set. Doing so will encourage them to stay with you, progress their careers, save money and reduce staff turnover. Sir Richard Branson is often quoted that, we should train our people well so they can leave but also treat them well so they don't want to.

Assessing the right ones

When you have a growing company, you need people who will grow with you, not hold you back. The people you hire will fall into three categories: those you can't believe how lucky you are to have found, disaster hires who do not fit with your business, your team or its values (and need to be removed fast), and the vast majority in between. This is the group that takes up most of your time; managing them, encouraging them, developing them. When people fit the culture, they are worth taking time over and persevering till you find them the right niche where they can flourish.

A similar entrepreneurial viewpoint comes from Australian tech entrepreneur Matt Bullock. Matt moves fast and wants the people around him to move fast too. Some people grow with that, and others hold the company back. The outstanding one's flourish. Matt has developed a process that all his employees have to go through every day to hone their thought processes. Everyone shares any new ideas they might have, or any problems or issues, be they with customers, suppliers or colleagues, and they then move on to share what they did that day and what they plan to do next. It is revealing and, of course, not everyone will thrive in this atmosphere.

When people are worth developing

Jamie Irwin, who runs an internet marketing company called Straight Up Search, passionately believes that training and development are worth the extra time you put into it them in the long run, providing you identify early on anyone who is not a good fit. Jamie gave me two examples. First, there was Joe, who was brilliant at video editing and production, with a YouTube channel of his own with over 50,000 subscribers. Jamie snapped him up for what would be Joe's first taste of employment. But while focusing on the skills, Jamie had not seen that Joe lacked the enthusiasm or soft skills required to fit in with the team. Many of us have employed a Joe, who wanders around, EarPods glued into their ears and avoiding eye contact at all costs. Jamie feels the responsibility was his, at least in part, for not providing enough introductory training on the expectations of employment and to have inspired Joe with a personal development plan.

A second hire, Holly, also had little experience in the workplace, having completed a Master's degree in Marketing, and started with Jamie as a general digital marketing assistant. This time, however, Jamie used video tools, regular video conferences and screen shares to bring her up to speed with new software tools to increase her productivity and output. He also worked with her on a Personal Development Plan and recognized a real desire to develop her skills. They are now looking at investing in paid digital marketing qualifications and sponsored trips to digital marketing conferences in her new specialist area, as Holly is now his PR and Content Strategist. This has been a case of enabling talent and developing it for the benefit of both sides.

Right person, wrong job

Another great story came to me from mother and son duo Sanjay and Shashi Aggarwal, who founded the Spice Kitchen brand in 2012. They had spent a long time looking for a Senior Administrator and PA and found someone who appeared to be the ideal person based solely on skills and experience. However, it very quickly became apparent that their new hire hated admin, and continually volunteered to help out in the warehouse to avoid it. Instead of rushing in and thinking "wrong hire," they watched and saw how this recruit flourished and re-organized the whole operation and warehouse. She led the pickers and packers' team and then ultimately led the transition to a new location, where she is now Operations Manager of that team.

Sanjay and Shashi found it was a lesson in flowing with the energy, watching where someone flourished, and playing to their strengths. This was a prime example of the right person but the wrong role. Sanjay and Shashi now apply the same techniques in recruitment. They look for the right person who fits, loves the business and is passionate, bringing positive energy and a drive to do a fantastic job, and the rest then slots into place. They have learned that people are way more than a list of competencies, and they give space for new hires to bring 'all' of themselves to the role rather than restrict them by being rigid about how suited a particular person is to a role.

The Pitfalls

In the same way as you can miss out by rigidly enforcing your needs, to keep someone in a job they clearly loathe, training and developing them for the company's needs alone doesn't work either. Take note of Jamie working with Holly on her personal development plan (PD). PDPs should focus on where people want to go, what skills they want to add, what direction they want their career to go. It is not about you or the company. When people feel they are going in the direction they choose, then they will feel that they matter.

Avoid the pitfall of promoting to suit the company too. Take a scenario where someone is thriving in their job, your best designer, for example. Connor (for the sake of argument) is the perfect example of company values embodied, brilliant at designing, the star of the department. So, when your current manager leaves, it is obvious that you should promote Connor. Isn't it?

The short answer is no. Just because Connor is brilliant at his job as a designer does not mean he would be a competent manager, which involves an entirely different skill set. Equally, Connor may well love his job as a designer and have absolutely no desire to be a manager. Instead, you briskly wade in and forcing the promotion through will leave you with a poor manager, with whom you will eventually have to part company, having lost your best designer in the process. Disaster all round.

If you have a robust process from day one of finding out what your team members want out of their job and career, short and mid-term, you can regularly align their goals to the company's goals rather than enforce something they don't want, that doesn't suit them. You would know in advance that Connor would never fit the manager role, and aim to help Connor develop his design skills even further, which can only benefit the company. What you then get is a win-win instead. Training and development are not about what suits the company, but rather what suits the person. Happy people make successful companies.

Staying Relevant And Out Of Trouble

We have seen the speed with which tech has developed over the last couple of years. So, we will have a look at how much impact this should have on a not-predominantly tech business, which aspects of tech you need to find solutions for, and which might be ok to ignore.

Something else that has always been an under-rated challenge but has come into focus for many businesses during the pandemic is supply chains. Delays and rising costs have become a nightmare for many. How do your de-risk a supply chain – and talking of risks, how well protected are you from the unexpected? Systems make many entrepreneurs yawn, yet they are essential to growth and to help protect your business if something takes you out of the equation for a while. Another much discussed concept over the last couple of years has been agility. Do you give up if your markets disappear, or do you adapt and change – and thrive?

Lots of things will help the smooth running of your business, while building value and enabling you being able to step away on a day-to-day basis. But it is easy to get blinded by all the advice and fall into the perfectionism trap.

There are only three questions you need to ask: do your customers love you, do your teams love working for you, and are you financially sustainable? If the answer to those three remains a huge and positive "yes" every time you check (and check regularly and often), you are 99% there already.

CHAPTER THIRTY SIX

Keeping up with the tech

Tech has become a world of extreme. For some companies, it something to dread, something too outside of their comfort zones, yet for others, it's a place where it is all too easy to spend several fortunes in the conviction that you need the most complex of everything.

But it is a case of remembering Michael Holmstrom's thoughts on innovation. Concentrate on any problem you want to solve, rather than assuming you can't do something – whilst also remembering that having a great business is still the most important thing.

Tech is only 5% of the problem

Ben Talin created a full-solution IT and Marketing company at 13 and had sold it by the time he was eighteen. He says that his ego was massive at that point, and he built two colossal platforms in the days before anything was big enough to be called a platform. Since then, he has had a succession of start-ups and is the founder of 361consult.com, and morethandigital.info, one of the world's most prominent initiatives for digitalization, innovation, and futurist topics. As an ambassador for a digital future and consultant for change, his opinion is sought by companies and governments alike.

Ben's consultancy helps clients find a sustainable and long-term route to becoming successful, turn-arounds being one of his specialist areas. They believe in a holistic approach and, to my fascination, say that only 5% of the work they are needed to do is specifically technology.

Tech is always an enabler and a tool rather than a solution. Cultural change is equally crucial for technology to be effective, and they have to become the change agent. Ben says that everyone asks him the same question, "how can we get ourselves/companies/countries to go more digital" when they should be asking "how should we use our potential."

The following story is simple but outlines this confusion over tech always being the necessary solution. Ben and his team were called into a mid-size company to build an e-commerce shop. He quickly found out that the company was not "digital-ready". When Ben asked about the overall digitalization efforts, they told him, "Ah, yes, we got some new computers last year." And yes, there were servers and computers everywhere. The real problem wasn't that they needed a website shop but that none of their processes had been integrated, and everything ended in an old system with many points of friction and mistakes.

Ben sees this so often. In this case, paperwork, including the orders, went through several departments. Each page would be printed off at some point, with a copy made later by someone else. But of course, they had "always done it this way". No one had asked the obvious question 'why not pre-set the first printer to automatically set two copies", which would result in half of the effort expended in the previous process, and half the room for error.

Meanwhile, orders for this company's steel T-bars were coming in from construction sites in hand-written notes. These orders had to be transcribed and were often interpreted wrongly due to people's writing. Sometimes they were incredibly urgent, but the people in-house couldn't read them and had to try and get hold of the right person on site, which invariably they couldn't, which caused delays.

Ben's team created a QR code for each product for the people on construction sites to order via an app. Ben says he had never realized how many versions of steel appliances there are! The people on the sites immediately had all the details on the app to ensure they were ordering the right T-Bar with the correct dimensions and alloy for their job, and the whole supply process could then be automated. It became so smooth that not only were there no more mistakes in the distribution, but this company was able to deliver the same day, beating all their competition in time and efficiency. So, they achieved not a webstore but an entire customer experience transformation by focusing on the processes and delivery that mattered – not the tech.

This story is a simple yet potent example of how companies need to address tech to beat the competition and not just buy into fancy and expensive salesmanship. Bear in mind Ben's five percent rule and concentrate on what matters.

The VR Revolution

Sometimes things are easier to teach yourself than you might expect. One example of that is VR videos, which have become an accessible business asset to bring what you do to life and completely overhaul your marketing. Yet they are just one step up from using ordinary video. There is an extensive choice of cameras that film in panoramic mode and many do the stitching together for you. For a professional look, you may still have to do a bit of editing here or there with some video editing software. However, the difference in impact is vast, and more and more people now have VR glasses so they can take full advantage of the experience you offer.

Compelling videos tell stories, and you need to develop reasons to inspire people to want to look around and experience the whole video. Without the hook, they won't bother, but that is, of course, no different than any other marketing.

Armchair Travel

Sway PR founder Mark Hayward became interested in VR a few years ago, and it quickly became a pet passion. He knew that the time would come when flat images would become redundant, and we would move to a more interactive format. With Facebook and the Metaverse and Google and Microsoft racing to produce their own versions, the move to virtual environments is accelerating fast.

Mark's first foray was to buy an inexpensive VR camera to play around with. Five years ago, it cost a few hundred pounds, and worked through an app on your mobile. It was fun, and whilst the images were good enough quality for social media, they were a bit grainy for anything else.

When COVID hit, Mark had some more time to research VR to see if he could develop it further, which would add another service for his PR clients and offer more value to journalists. He invested in a professional VR setup including a Cannon D6 camera with a fisheye lens that could produce images at a 180-degree arc. Images are then stitched together to give the full VR effect. Mark then set about capturing the world around him to test out its capabilities. He was hooked.

The Travel industry, a specialist area for Sway PR, is being revolutionized by Virtual Reality with a few of Mark's friends and associates taking the object of his passion to a new level. One, from Lights Over Lapland created unforgettable 360-degree videos of Lapland during the lockdown, including a stunning experience under the Northern Lights. Despite travel being impossible, using a VR experience, the business grew massively, which was almost unheard of in the travel industry during COVID.

Another of Mark's clients, Off the Map Travel, started with putting virtual experiences on their website, and seeing its success, the owner founded a ground-breaking new business, Virtually Visiting. Their users create their own virtual passports and can visit guided tours in countries around the world, from an Arctic tour to the Louvre or the plains of Africa – all in an afternoon. Virtually Visiting uses the best local tour guides to create the experiences and share in the revenue. Now armchair travel is a "virtual" reality.

A cautionary tale

Bhairav Patel is MD of Atom CTO, a group whose core focus is to provide technology advice to start-ups. Bhairav says they continually see horror stories involving people putting all their money into tech and not getting anything close to what they hoped for.

One company came to them, desperate, needing a product finished in three months. Yet the work required would take a year, at least. This company's next round of funding was subject to the product being delivered, so it was desperate times for them.

They had hired an overseas team whom they had never met to build the platform, and been reassured by the management that everything was fine for six months. With three months to go, they discovered this overseas company did not even have a developer team in place. It emerged that they had tried to hire a team for the first few months and then patched together people from other projects in a hurry, so the product at that point had little or nothing to do with what had been ordered. By the time they came to Bhairav for help, they had no money left, nor the year of development time that the job needed.

Bhairav says to always do the proper diligence on the companies that are working for you and that if there are deadlines that the business depends on, then make sure you emphasise them to the companies that are working for you. One way you can ensure that projects are on track is to ask for regular updates. Especially in tech, you must be able to see results on a regular basis. Never blindly trust that things will be delivered.

Overall conclusions

Tech without a financial return is a waste of time and a business disaster waiting to happen. Some massive changes can be achieved surprisingly easily. It is vital to look at the complete picture of what you are trying to achieve, every process, and the what and the why behind it. And to keep everything simple.

Worry less about snazzy tech and more about ensuring the customer is happy with the journey, and never spend more than you can afford while still having a viable business. Don't be afraid of tech; you might well be able to surprise yourself and do far more than you had dreamed yourself.

CHAPTER THIRTY SEVEN

AI, 3D, Machine Learning

I f VR is within reach of us all, how about ML, AI and 3D? Will we all jump onto the metaverse? All things tech are leaping forward at an astonishing rate. Neuromorphic computing is working on imitating the structure of the human brain. AI is becoming faster and improving all the time. There may come a time when a humanoid robot is indeed indistinguishable from a human in the metaverse. But not only are we not fully there yet, but these technologies are outside the scope of most businesses.

However, that does not mean that nearly every business benefits or could benefit from AI and machine learning, and we can find so much to progress on open source (publicly accessible). Humanity can benefit hugely in so, so many ways from some of this work, from business, healthcare and defence, to entertainment. Many of us are concerned with ethics, and the ethical way forward is as much open to collaboration as possible. Transparency and trust are always better for humanity, and also great for businesses searching the web in need of the vast amount of help there is already available.

Amplifying your business with AI

Anything World was co-founded by Gordon Midwood and offers

a platform to build interactive 3D experiences faster and better using machine learning and AI. Gordon is a programmer and serial games developer whose idea is to make everyone capable of becoming a content creator.

There are so many areas of development in tech right now, and it is easy to think you should be involved in all of them. Gordon's advice is to stick to what is relevant to the core of what you do and ignore anything else. Just because, for example, NFTs attract investment doesn't mean that they are relevant to your company. It is always crucial to be cautious about trends.

AI and machine learning are influencing nearly everything in our daily lives. It may be through Siri or Alexa, your car predicting a possible accident, automated emails in your style, or for some of us, creating entire 3D Worlds. Reviews influence our buying habits and affect our success far more than we think. There are the obvious tools such as voice assistants, but there is also so much on offer in the creative space that wasn't on offer two years ago. Gordon says that Anything World democratizes creativity by sharing and encouraging that knowledge.

Gordon believes that, as a tech start-up, you develop an MVP and have to walk a narrow line between promoting your vision and exaggerating the truth. Partly this comes from the fact that investors want to be absolutely convinced about whether they will see a return before investing. Gordon feels that this system encourages over-promising.

In the same way, you have to balance your fear of failure with your belief in the end product. Like many tech companies, they knew what they set out to do would work in theory after nearly a year of research, but they wouldn't be able to find out whether it worked in practice almost until the pre-alpha release. You often don't know a live demo will work until the crucial moment. Gordon and his co-founder experienced this when they had to fly out to a potential investor in the States with no idea if their demo would work properly or if they would be coming home in shame. These particular investors insisted on seeing something visual.

I asked Gordon how someone could enhance their business in these areas with relatively little skill. He says reading around the subject is a good start, and hiring specialists is even better. But Machine Learning engineers earn incredible amounts and are way beyond the reach of start-ups. They partnered with a London university, got to know them well, and hired three postgrads as interns for three months. All three stayed on at the end, bringing the needed talent and the passion that inspires others. Gordon maintains that he doesn't always know what he is doing but finds it is possible to thrive by working it out as you do it.

The vital role of open-source in ethics

Richard Boyd has had an extraordinary career and is recognized as a global expert in AI, ML, and 3D. Starting in the pre-internet days, he worked in film, computer gaming, and 3D design tools. He says he has "tilted at the windmills of virtual reality, Augmented Reality, Artificial Intelligence, and Machine Learning", and that he came to believe early that humans and machines would cooperate to build a more promising future.

When Lockheed Martin bought Richard's computer game technology company, Richard went to work for them for a few years and created his own lab called Virtual World Labs. They were trying to solve huge problems, from space travel to robotic systems and cyber threats with 100-year-old machinery and systems. Richard became Director of Emerging and Disruptive Technologies and set out to harness networked intelligence. The graphical internet had shown what happens with a system with clear rules and simple steps for people to follow, and it accelerated the information age as we know it today. Linus Torvalds designed the heart of Linux and made it easy for people to contribute through open-source. Companies raced to profit from open source, and Red Hat software is the most prominent capitalization at this point in time.

Richard also drew from Dee Hock's creation, Visa International. Conceptually, it was a very non-traditional company, conceived before the internet yet aiming to build the largest financial organization in the world. Dee Hock used what he called Chaordia, a system that was a balance between rigid, controlled, or archaic, and fluid systems. They do not issue credit cards but simply provide the IT for others to do so.

In 2009, the then Secretary of Defence in the US named escalating healthcare costs one of the top threats to National Security. With his team from Lockheed, Richard toured hospitals and healthcare companies. Among the many things they found was the lack of using basic engineering principles such as checklists, simulations training, safety interlocks, alarm management, and systems engineering. $120 trillion was estimated to be lost in annual waste and $300 billion in medical errors. Richard and his team designed an open-source hierarchical simulation architecture named ICESTORM to model every process, piece of equipment, healthcare intervention, and human activity from when someone is ill or injured until they leave their hospital bed and return home. They used existing data and estimated when none was available. Because it was all open-source, it could, they hoped, continue to be regularly added to as the information became available.

ICESTORM is buried in the archives now, but Richard hopes that some parts of it are being used on other programmes within the thriving military healthcare system. As it was being wound down, he learned that defining a contribution system for tech is not enough. Richard believes that we have to make clear inducements for people to do so. Those who discover new drugs or invent new devices are incentivized to guard them until they are patented and protected. If only this could change to incentivize them to join in open and full collaboration and work together on systems to help conquer disease, injury, and aging.

Simulation-based 3D Internet

Richard and his team also designed an open-source system for simulation called the Virtual World Framework, which still survives today. The sponsor was the Under Secretary of Defence for training, readiness, and strategy, and they were looking for a new standard for military simulations. He wanted "internet age innovation."

Once again, the team used open-sourced systems. The VWF can still be found on Wikipedia and GitHub[1] so that millions of inventors can continue to try to solve humanity's most pressing issues. They see the VWF ecosystem multiplying and taking new directions in the same way as the internet did in its early days. It could very well serve as the core of the metaverse. They also believe that, if properly managed, non-specialists will be empowered to create simulations, learning, and other content and applications.

Richard says significant issues such as disease, old age, global weirding (extreme climate changes), space travel, renewable energy, famine, and water scarcity - these can only be solved through this approach. Simulating ideas and designs with a huge

---

1   http://en.wikipedia.org/wiki/Virtual_world_framework

parallel contribution systems tied to incentives then both help people prosper alongside solving the problems. That is a recipe that will ensure the survival of humanity.

All of this makes for an incredibly exciting time to be starting a business in this field. We have to continue to balance progress with ethics, work on finding our own solutions and encouraging open source.

CHAPTER THIRTY EIGHT

Supply Chains

The importance of supply chains varies from business to business. For any product-based business, they are critical and can present a dramatic risk to your business, as so many companies have discovered. With shortages worldwide, logistics routes closed down, and transport costs doubling, many companies have had to scramble to find alternative and more sustainable suppliers on shore.

Manufacturing is challenging to make reliable at the best of times with so much potential for going wrong. Setting yourself up is massively costly, and with sub-contracting, many existing manufacturers are not interested in small customers, being geared to mass production instead. The smaller, less automated manufacturers may be keen to get the work, but they are also more vulnerable to problems of their own.

How do you start when no one knows you?

When Daniel Flynn, Jarryd Burns and Daniel's now wife Justine co-founded the Australian social enterprise, Thankyou, they set out with huge dreams to change the world. They chose bottled water as their first product, but with no idea how to start a bottled water company, they resorted to Google.

It became clear that creating a unique bottle could cost over $150,000, and they would need at least two-thirds of that just to start the first run. Start-up costs were going to add up to over a quarter of a million dollars. With about a thousand dollars between them, they knew it wasn't going to happen that way.

They decided to approach existing manufacturers to supply them instead. They managed to secure some meetings, but these proved challenging to say the least. Daniel would borrow a smart suit from his dad, and he and Jarryd would have to park their slightly battered old cars mixed in with glossy new Porches and Mercedes in the corporate lots.

Every manufacturer would tell them how hard it would be to launch a new brand of water, assuring them the market was challenging to enter and nigh on impossible to succeed in. These experienced manufacturers would look at the two of them and question them as to what their unique marketing angle was. Their only option was to appear confident and sweep the questions away, announcing that such details were confidential but what they needed to know was if the manufacturers could handle the capacity of orders they would need.

It was much the same story discussing minimum orders, where nods had to suffice for assurances from the pair. Their major panic was struggling with the technical terms that they didn't understand and had to scribble down in order to surreptitiously look up later.

Quality issues and product recalls:

Placing orders was only one of Thankyou's early challenges. Their first order was sent directly from their manufacturer to the huge distributor, MBC, who had given them their first big break.

Wanting to see the product for themselves, they excitedly greeted the arrival of one pallet at Daniel's parents' garage. The initial, excited chatter turned to deadly hush as the packaging was pulled away. There were bottles with creased and crumpled labels in every box they opened. It would transpire that around a third were affected. When they contacted the manufacturer, the quality control person was on holiday, but they quickly established that the entire run had been affected.

MBC had already sent the product out across Australia. Every bottle had to be recalled. While the supplier covered the recall cost, the sales profit was lost. It is a testament to the Thankyou team that they not only kept going but have turned the brand into the success it is, with their personal care products now stocked by major retailers across Australia and New Zealand.

Mitigating the risks

You are exposed to colossal risk in any supplier's hands as an early-stage business, as they will have far more important customers demanding their attention. It will cost them far less in financial penalties and reputation to let you down, but for you, it could mean letting down all your customers, leaving your reputation in tatters. It always pays to invest heavily in researching your prospective supplier. Ideally, speak to other customers and verify the reviews.

The better you know your market, the more you will understand what you need from a supplier. Considerations over and above the goods or services themselves might include public liability insurance, health and safety protection, or a standards accreditation in your industry in addition to the product itself. Even assuming you acquire all of these, still do spot checks yourself on the quality regularly. A supplier that produced brilliantly last year may have run into trouble this year.

Building up a relationship with your supplier is crucial. This should be a partnership, so show that you are someone they would want a long-term relationship with. The better you know them, and the stronger your relationship, the harder it will be for you to be the customer they let down when they are in a jam. So, spend time with them, talk to them as people, outside transactions, on a regular basis.

Transparency on both sides leads to trust and joint decisions in achieving the best outcomes on both cost and quality. The process of forming a contract needs to be one undertaken in complete good faith. The best suppliers are partners who know your plans and view the prospect of you doing well as something that will also benefit them. The more they identify with your goals and values, the more they will buy into and share your business goals. Your suppliers should be one of your biggest assets.

The cheapest supplier may look appealing, but if quality affects your standards, deciding to go with them may be costly in the end. Reliability, honesty, and trust are worth paying a little extra for. And, of course, you should always carry out periodic cost reviews. It is all too easy to let these slip and become part of a crisis management cost-cutting exercise rather than routine. Regular reviews mean you have time to assess and, if need be, find new suppliers. Never fear taking that step, though be sure to try and work with your existing suppliers first.

In the same way, you also need to review your products regularly. It is easy to hang on to items in your line that you feel emotionally attached to for one reason or another, convincing yourself they will soon sell more again. Stringent, data-based supplier reviews stop the temptation to hang on to dead wood or be caught with a large stock of unsellable items.

The nearer your supplier's location, the less risk, and the more sustainable they are. Diversification of your suppliers also waters down risk. But that is a balancing act in that the more business you give someone, the higher priority you will be, while on the other hand, no back-up means total exposure. Supply chains are full of unexpected hiccups, and you need to build resilience to those. Regularly ask yourself what would happen to your business if each or, indeed, every supply chain broke down. What things can you foresee that might upset supply; even seasonal changes to weather or labour supply can have a gargantuan impact on business. Always have back-up plans.

CHAPTER THIRTY NINE

Systems

Systems are a subject that, for entrepreneurs, really divide the crowd. For many entrepreneurs, impatient, big picture people, the mere word is a massive yawn. But remember the Pete Drucker quote, "if you can't measure it, you can't manage it"...

Why Systems Matter

Dave Jenyns is the founder of Systemology and is all about making systems easy. He has also launched systemHUB to help other entrepreneurs systemize easily, learning from his own entrepreneurial experiences. In addition, he has written the book Systemology with a foreword by Michael Gerber. Both of them believe in systems, and Dave explained to me that the reason that they are anathema to many entrepreneurs, springs from a series of misconceptions. Because of those misplaced beliefs, systems never reach the top of the to-do list and so can cause businesses deeply problematic issues.

In the early stages, lack of systems can mean constant fire-fighting, large amounts of time wasted sorting out problems, and a general lack of control over outcomes. If one central member of staff leaves, if everything they do and the way they do it is written down, the business isn't suddenly going to hit a crisis. But if not, you could be facing just that.

Another of those misconceptions is that there is no point in setting up a system until you've reached the point of perfection. Dave says that is like McDonald's waiting to be where they are now.

Systems should be easy to update

Some people only truly focus on systems when they come to sell a business. David gave me the example of Jeanette Farron of Diggiddy Doggy Daycare, a multi-award-winning dog care centre. She had always planned to sell and, aware of the importance of systems and documentation, had been diligent in keeping everything updated herself, originally. Thirteen years in, the pressure of the business was taking its toll, and Jeanette felt it was the time to sell.

Checking those systems and accounts were "sale-ready," Jeanette found them all over the place. Unfortunately, the original systems she had set up with such care weren't easy to access, so the team had not refined or improved them over the years. Once they resolved these issues, Jeanette stopped working full time, worked on the business, and in time sold it for more than she had anticipated.

Dave always recommends starting with the critical systems. Entrepreneurs often try to avoid starting, but Dave argues that it doesn't have to be the owner who sets up the systems after the first one. Once their critical client flow has been established, done by documenting one client, one product and one journey to give you this, you have the basis of your plan and it can be extended by someone else within the company may well enjoy that type of work.

Sales without systems = disaster

Jake Munday is an entrepreneur who found success via social media. At 23, he purchased a Facebook page called "Dog Lovers", which he managed to quickly grow from 440k followers to over 4 million likes. Affiliate sales brought in $40,000 a month, and he was hooked. He sold the page in 2014 to US investors. Other ventures have followed, and currently, his focus is with Custom Neon, co-founded with his wife, Jess. They were looking for a custom neon sign for their new-born son's bedroom, which resulted in them identifying a gap in the market that they could fill. They started an Instagram page and another new company with a $500 investment. Customer Neon is now a $10 million global business with offices in London, Australia, and the US.

Jake forewarns of a trap I fell into regularly when I had businesses – concentrating all your focus on the sales figures. He says that when you are full of ideas and enthusiasm, you start and move forward at such a fast pace that you are reluctant to put the brakes on. It is easy to push too hard, increase ad spend, and hire reactively to capitalize on sales. He admits that in his early career, he would neglect to consider the impact of this on supply, delivery, customer service, and fulfilment. They were making the sales but also apologizing for products being out of stock. There were also inconsistencies in team training, processes, and policies, leading to an unsatisfactory customer experience.

Jess provides balance and champions the 80/20 management principle both in business and life, which helps them clarify their goals and reminds them not to sweat the small stuff. One of those 80/20 rules is that 80% of your revenue will come from 20% of your customers. The moment you realize just that one fact, it focuses you on prioritizing that 20% and ensuring that they stay with you for the long-term.

Jake says that he has learned from previous experience that bouncing around from idea to idea without due diligence and structured monitoring can lead to team whiplash, stress, and decreased productivity. Jess, together with their operations manager, provides a more methodical approach and are instrumental in creating harmony, trust, and unity amongst the team. Jake says that much as he wants to push forward, he knows how to be more strategic and play to their strengths. Now he also focuses on ways to streamline processes, reduce costs, manage logistics, integrate global communications and CRM systems, and provide comprehensive, uniformed staff training across their international branches. Jake found out the hard way that drilling down to lay the foundations for sustained steady growth will ultimately lead to more success, happiness, and longevity in our businesses.

KPIs

Systems cover a multitude of sins but many are there to set out how things are best done. Systems for measuring how you are performing (KPIs or key performance indicators) are even more crucial. The operative word is key. You can spend all your time measuring irrelevant things, but it is the main results that matter.

KPIs are a way of focusing on the headlines of the business overall, while department heads might prioritise the headlines of their departments. The more accurate KPIs you have, the easier life becomes, and you can plan with more confidence because you have more control and more accurate data.

You have to find the right things to measure for you and your business. What is essential in one business may not be as crucial in another, but financial performance alongside team and customer happiness are toplines. A personalized KPI dashboard keeps you in control.

Overall

There can be downsides to systems. Teams flourish with automation but also need to be creative, and feel encouraged to make their own contributions. If you are entirely automated, making everything processed works fine. If you are dealing with humans, a little less control is required to get the best from people.

Systems have to make sense to the people who use them. Otherwise, all you are creating is something that will sit in a drawer or a folder and never be used. Worse, you may base your decisions on resulting misinformation. For example, a CRM or even an accounts programme is only as good as the information that goes into it. So, if a quarter of – for example – your salespeople are sloppy about putting the finer points into the system, then everything you do is based on inaccurate data.

Equally, in a fast-growing business, the systems must be flexible to cope with the changes that will continually take place. When you are developing a business, you are forever changing the original plan, so no sooner than you tell people what is going on, it all changes. Systems have to fit every stage and be continually adaptable for change. Rigidity has no place in fast growth. Never be afraid to break and re-form your business and your systems; be sure your team are involved and buy into the need for them.

CHAPTER FORTY

Managing the Risks

Somewhere around 2015, I was on a high-growth course, of which one afternoon was devoted to business risks. It was an exceptional seminar, held by someone with a background in advising both global corporations and governments on risks. But, more importantly, the instructor knew how to grab an audience with a good mix of serious information and entertaining stories.

So it was, when I went back home, I pondered his insistence that we all consider what we would do if some "really bad flu" hit our businesses for a few weeks. At that time, I thought about it, and decided we could cope for two or three weeks if that extremity happened. Even businesses that made more detailed "flu" plans most probably still had nothing appropriate for COVID.

Financial Risk

When you are in trouble, but have a good sales platform, advisors will tend to tell you to keep going, restructure or look for a fire sale. If your product or service is selling, that is not a dead business, just one in a mess that someone from the outside can probably sort out.

Of course, what happened with the pandemic is that previously extremely healthy markets dried up overnight, so businesses were left without sales. Founders had to decide if they could keep going indefinitely, perhaps with government loans, with no business. The wise ones pivoted to a lesser or greater extent. While borrowing money might bring short-term relief, creditors were always going to come banging on the door again and no-one could be sure when the old markets would return, if at all.

The problem is that we humans fear the unknown, and outcomes of dramatic change are always unknown. So, when faced with it, we tend to freeze and do nothing, which is the worst possible option to take. We have to face the fear and work out the steps to success and then focus on them one at a time, achieving little by little. A specialist advisor can be a great help, and it is critical to get advice if you are trading insolvently to ensure you don't break any laws.

Diversity of customer base even when a market is healthy protects you, but only if your systems stop any single client from running up too high a bill. Having too many eggs in one basket is asking for trouble. Also in that seminar, we discussed another big risk; theft and fraud by employees. These are often not reported because no company wants it made known that they have been easy to take for a ride. But it is common. I certainly had more than one case of it, and I am far from alone.

No-one is immune

Damian Conolly FCCA is MD of Sakura Business Solutions Ltd. He was the Group Financial Controller in a fast-growing UK property investment/services business before the 2008 crash. They had set up a joint venture business in Hong Kong. Although it was in their name and they had responsibilities for overseeing the growth and development of the business, the office was being run on a day-to-day basis by the local directors.

These directors had recruited a local finance team from people they had worked with previously. They were supposed to report to the Head Office in the UK, but little real information was forthcoming from their Management Accountant nearly a year in. The accountant was complaining about being overworked, having a lack of support, yet providing poor and very generic information about what was happening at the Hong Kong end.

Uneasy, Damian, and his colleague raised it with both UK and Hong Kong directors but were told that this man was doing a great job. Eventually, Damian suggested one of them fly out to check but was told there was no budget for it. The day came when they got an emergency call saying the Hong Kong management accountant had disappeared, taking his laptop, some cash, and leaving chaos and a trail of angry suppliers behind him.

After spending two weeks in Hong Kong with the Group Finance Director, Damian had established that no accounting work had been done, but there had been systematic theft of office equipment and cash. On top of all that, it was found that the company credit card had been used for stays in 5-star hotels across Asia for him with a variety of women, and incredibly these trips had been charged to the business for a second time as personally incurred business expenses.

From that time on, Damian was very closely involved with the recruitment of a replacement and their supervision – and the finance team's concerns were listened to.

Other Risks

Risks don't stop at finance and pandemics. There is cyber fraud to consider. There are all the weather-related ones, from storm damage to loss of production, which may or may not be covered by insurance. Fire probably will be – but not for the amount it will cost you. We also have to consider the possibility of war or terror attacks. I remember discussing if our drivers had a plan to get home from major cities we distributed to all over the UK in the case of attack, something that had never occurred to me.

Compliance risks are enormous for most countries these days. Laws are increasingly onerous and complex, and it is easy to fall foul of one and end up with a huge fine. There is reputation risk. We have seen many successful companies suffer from a high-profile online attack by a group of ex-employees. The attacks may or may not have justification – but the damage to reputation will be vast and costly in either case.

Many businesses can withstand one of these issues but some suffer, by bad luck, a perfect storm of them. If several hit in a short space of time, it can be just too much to recover from. Bad luck happens to business owners too, but you can only call it that if you are genuinely sure you took every step you could to protect the business.

It is a balance of taking all the possible precautions you can, and accepting that sometimes, life is out of your control. But equally, sometimes risk brings opportunity.

Risks bring opportunity

Glen Bhimani is both founder and CEO of BPS Security, one of the fastest-growing security firms in the US. Glen says that keeping up with current political and world events can be extremely tricky as a busy entrepreneur – more so than ever in a world where the wrong public statement can destroy your reputation, and even magnanimous acts can be misinterpreted.

Glen developed a habit of keeping a close eye on world economics and events. This close eye turned into a more in-depth study in December 2019, looking at how COVID-19 impacted the security industry in every country it spread to. He could see that the pandemic was beginning to cause a strain on his sector, with buildings being abandoned with expensive equipment still in them. The security industry was struggling to keep up, and Glen knew a supply chain issue would arise as soon as COVID-19 made it to America. So, at the end of that December, Glen placed large orders for equipment supplies, including batons, vests, and more, and began interviewing substantial numbers of potential guards.

When the virus hit the United States, the security industry began to buckle as it had in other countries. But because Glen and his team had prepared by getting their supplies and starting interviews before it ever actually happened, they thrived. When buildings began to be abandoned and the demand for security shot through the roof, they could step up and fill that need.

Thanks to keeping an eye on current events and focussing how they impacted their industry, the company managed to grow by over 400% in the second quarter of 2020. Glen's story is an excellent example of how, by keeping an eye on current events, you can avoid disaster and fill gaps when your industry is struggling, create opportunities for significant growth in your company.

CHAPTER FORTY ONE

Pivoting

Pivoting has become one of the buzzwords in the last couple of years, but the principle has been part of business strategy for a great deal longer than that. Some argue the case for Wrigley's chewing gum being an early pivot. Mr. Wrigley Junior was working as a salesman and came up with the idea of giving away gum to entice customers to buy his soap and baking powders. But when the gum proved far more popular, they pivoted and made it their main product, and Wrigley's is now the monumentally successful company we know today.

One company that has pivoted twice, each time with increased success, is Netflix. Netflix started life by posting out DVDs to rent. At the time, most towns had a DVD rental shop, but Netflix offered more choice, and it was easier and cheaper, so it was a classic case of playing to customers' pain points. Netflix always had plans to stream, and once the technology was in place, DVD hire became a minor side project. Then, Netflix became a creator of content with a further pivot a few years later, and we all know how phenomenally successful they are in that space today.

A lesser-known pivot is that of Twitter. Twitter started life as Odeo, a podcasting platform. But when iTunes appeared, they lost traction and re-invented themselves as Twitter. Twitter's team had just a short time to brainstorm a whole new concept to revolutionize the company, unlike Netflix's more planned progression. A pivot is usually a drastic change of direction, as Twitter did, when what you are offering doesn't appeal to the markets anymore.

When the pandemic arrived, it wasn't a case of products and services not appealing to the marketplace as much as it being completely impossible for many companies to provide them. Lockdowns meant people couldn't come to work. Some sectors were lucky in already being able to work online, or to make a comparatively easy transition. Others required something much more drastic to survive.

I have heard many extraordinary pandemic pivoting stories that picking a few to share was almost impossible. I think the common denominators during this time are the grit, the determination, the refusal not to save personal skin, but the livelihoods of others that touch me the most. But these also provide inspiration and examples of how you can use an existing company to service new markets as the need arises.

Pivoting to help her hometown

Calypso Rose is a UK entrepreneur, founder of Indytute, a successful experiences business, and previously ITV's Young Business Person of the Year. In the first spring of the pandemic, it became evident that theirs would be one of the sectors worst hit. They struggled to find their feet transferring to zoom, but nevertheless found the time and energy to raise money for a food distribution charity.

If losing 90% of your business isn't bad enough, two weeks into lockdown, Calypso was cycling down a quiet country road when her small son in front put down his leg unexpectedly. Her son was fine. Calypso broke her jaw in five places, lost a few teeth, and had to have emergency surgery. She says that if you struggle with zoom, you need to try it lisping through wires.

It didn't stop her. Calypso has a very close bond with her partners, all of whom were suffering the same loss of business. So, they worked on changing their experiences into boxed kits that could be enjoyed at home. This pivot proved a massive success.

Calypso also saw that her local town of Deal in Kent was being annihilated, from the farmers' markets to craft shops, cafes, and the local artisans. On the last Saturday before the first lockdown, while many people were in panic mode, Calypso was out establishing which businesses could offer delivery. Self-funding, she set up Dealdelivers.com, which was live within a week. She says Amazon appears to be forgotten in Deal. Everyone is shopping locally, and businesses are thriving. Since then, Calypso has also helped other people set up their own regional hubs elsewhere.

From Stages to Furniture

Another sector to have been annihilated at the start of the pandemic were the businesses supplying the events industry. Australian entrepreneurs Tabitha and Jeremy Fleming had built Stagekings to offer custom-designed stages. They had accrued an impressive portfolio of successes, including making much of the 2018 Commonwealth Games Opening Ceremony set. In March 2020, they were in the middle of building a truss structure for the Ninja Warrior film set, a set for Formula 1 in Melbourne, and a giant steel spherical cricket ball for the T-20 World Cup.

Every single booking they had for 2020 was cancelled within 48 hours due to COVID. Jeremy immediately called a team meeting, and they brainstormed survival tactics trying to second guess what people might need in the coming months. They had space, machinery, and skills, so they settled on making furniture. Overseas supplies were already drying up, and people needed to set up home offices.

Over that first weekend, they had two designs and were building prototypes. By Tuesday, they had finished a photo shoot and had a new eCommerce site up and running. They called the new company IsoKings, a combination of isolation and the original name. Also, on that Tuesday, Jeremy posted an open letter on social media telling the story and saying what they were doing to save jobs. The story went viral, and orders poured in.

Their original plan hoped to achieve orders of a hundred desks a month. Within three days, they were taking orders for three hundred a day. They were able to bring back all their original crew and hire more from out-of-work event crews. Roadies did the initial deliveries. They expanded their market to include retail and wholesale, equipment for schools, and educational games. They provided work for one hundred and forty people through COVID and created a new, super successful business, all from that one weekend.

Changing both Model and Market

Asim Amin is the founder and CEO of Plumm, a workplace well-being provider. Just before the pandemic hit, he and his team had prepped for months for an investment round, and conversations already underway.

The pandemic changed everything, including the investment market, and valuations plummeted. Asim was faced with a choice.

He could carry on with the investment round and take the hit on the valuation or make some pivotal changes in the business to survive without funding and then raise at a later time.

Asim had faith in the business and the team and chose to restructure and not go the investment route. Firstly, they shifted from a pay-as-you-go model into a subscription model. Then, they took the massive decision of changing their B2C business into solely B2B.

As a result, Plumm experienced its greatest period of growth. In addition, they were later able to go back and seek funding for a much healthier valuation than the original one.

With or without a Pandemic

Consumer demand changes now faster than ever. Adapting, pivoting, and evolving has to be an essential part of any company's arsenal, not just due to pandemics. No part of your business can be excluded from reconsideration, be it the model, the method or the entire sector – and on a regular basis.

At any stage, including starting up, you may find the Grand Plan or Product isn't quite as robust as you thought. The secret is never to overcomplicate things, never entrench them. You are in business to listen to the customer and use your skills to meet whatever needs they have. If you do that, along with having an innovative culture, your chances of thriving in an uncertain world are vastly improved.

CHAPTER FORTY TWO

The Biggest Risks of All

While reading this, I hope that you have recognized a world you have been looking for: somewhere you belong. While a lot of the advice here is aimed at fast-growth businesses, I don't think it matters how and where you start a business as long as it is the right thing for you at that moment – you can, after all, pivot later.

There is a snobbishness now attached to entrepreneurship; that only very high-growth businesses can call themselves true entrepreneurs. I don't see it this way. That would overlook the entrepreneurship of the traders who hit the beaches in holiday islands, selling whatever they can produce or catch, to give just one example. Markets have long been the breeding ground of great entrepreneurs. So many started a market stall; Steve Smith of Poundland, Michael Marks of Marks and Spencer, and Lord Sugar are just a few. There are massive benefits to that approach. The worst that can happen with a market stall is that you fail to set it up one day and lose the money tied up in the rest of your stock. Then there are the bedroom start-ups, and the garage start-ups: Apple with Steve Jobs and Steve Wozniak, and Jeff Bezos with Amazon amongst them. Now, we have coaching gurus basing themselves wherever they chose in very different types of businesses.

Many people start a business because they want more control over their lives – when they work, how they work, and who they work with – and internet-based companies appear to be the ultimate example of this. Caveat, though – I know several internet entrepreneurs who post about their high-quality lifestyle while telling me they are down to their last pennies. Don't buy into that particular hype without a touch of cynicism.

What you do doesn't matter

You may have come across a great idea, a new invention, a way of looking at things that no one has thought of that makes you so excited that you can't wait to set up a business doing it. If you don't have a wild, original idea, rather than try and innovate something new, look for something that there is high demand for. Look at the top players in that market and how they are performing, and think what you could do differently, better or more uniquely, to blow that competition out of the market.

If it is an old idea or a new idea, the secret of success lies in cracking an offer that converts into a constant income stream. And that comes from talking to customers – before you start, as you start and every day after that.

Why loving what you do matters

Clarity on what you want in life and the business is crucial. The gurus have it right when they say we need to live our lives more by design and take control of the choices we make, but we also need to be aware of what those choices mean. For example, setting up a high-growth business with a fast-growing team will not bring you total freedom. Selling goods will still bring supply chain issues.

You will not make millions without hassle.

'Love what you do' has become a hackneyed piece of advice but do not overlook just how essential it is when it comes to running a business. Many entrepreneurs have said to me that if you love what you do, you will never work a day in your life. I think that is a stretch, but it takes you a long way towards where you want to be.

It is your passion to achieve the impact from your work that will make the biggest difference. And that passion has to be completely, authentically yours. Don't part with good money for advice on how to live a life that suits someone else. True purpose increases your resilience, makes sense of your decisions, and moves you forward to your destination.

The two big risks

Few entrepreneurs know much when they start, and even if they do, they still make mistakes. That doesn't matter. But, in addition to forgetting to listen to your customers, or not putting your team first, there are two other mistakes that are even more dangerous.

One: never forget that your primary purpose is to make money. Yes, you may be saving the world in some way, but unless you make a financially viable business, you won't be able to keep on saving it. Check you are financially viable regularly and keep this at the forefront of your mind.

Two: If for any reason the time comes that you don't love that business anymore, that is ok. In fact, it is completely normal. Relationships change. But as with any other relationship, staying in once you have fallen out of love with it will quickly turn things toxic. So have that plan B so that you can always be decisive and leave the business. Your B plan will be ready, your business worth selling. The world won't fall apart if you move on. Just enjoy being madly in love with your business, however long that lasts.